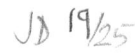

Finding Nell and Mads:
The Emotional Journeys of Two Rescue Dogs

Clare Cogbill

Copyright © 2023 Clare Cogbill

Cover Copyright © Connor McMorran

All rights reserved.

ISBN: 9798393320362

DEDICATION

For Nell and Mads.

And Ralph, whose journey intersected with theirs.

And, of course, Alun and Connor, who constantly go along with my mad ideas...

CONTENTS

Acknowledgments	i
Introduction	Pg 3
A Friend for Ralph	Pg 7
Enter Nell	Pg 16
Nell's Adoption Day	Pg 27
Getting to Know Nell	Pg 37
What on Earth Went Wrong?	Pg 46
Renovations and a Move	Pg 57
Living in the Country	Pg 74
Instincts	Pg 82
A New Canine Playmate	Pg 98
So, He's Staying Then?	Pg 111
A Breakthrough	Pg 122
Dogs 'Living Their Best Life'	Pg 131
Dogs: Our 'Reciprocal' Friendship	Pg 142
Tell Us What You Need, Mads!	Pg 149
Understanding the Dog Politics	Pg 161

Being Sighthound Guardians	Pg 167
Some Rescue Dogs Gone By	Pg 180
The New Team of Three	Pg 192
Lumps, Bumps, and the Girl Next Door	Pg 201
Rodents Again	Pg 210
Where Were You Before?	Pg 216
That Recall Problem	Pg 221
Dogs: When the End Arrives	Pg 226
Gotcha Day	Pg 236
And Now	Pg 242
And Onwards	Pg 249

ACKNOWLEDGMENTS

Thank you to all those who support me in my writing ventures, and the many rescue dogs whose stories have inspired me.

And to Connor McMorran for another great book cover.

INTRODUCTION

It was never my intention to write another dog book. The writing part of my brain had moved onto other things and was exploring other sorts of tales to tell. But when we found ourselves with two of our three dogs deceased, and two more rescue dogs had wandered into our lives, the experiences that followed influenced my writing journey – temporarily blocking out those other stories. And so, lo and behold, the story began all by itself and writing it became something I needed to do in order to clear my mind.

One thing that didn't happen in this book, however, was for me to find these two dogs' 'voices' which means everything in here is from my perspective. In previous books, Ralph, Peggy, and Lucy's voices came easily to me, hence I was able to imagine what they might have been thinking. Their voices were popular with most readers and not so with a few others, but it was the way their stories unfolded and imagining their inner voices became a part of that journey.

That has been difficult with Nell and Mads, perhaps because of the way in which this particular story's trajectory panned out? I really don't know.

As the events evolved, I thought more and more that writing about what happened might help some other people who were embarking on their journey with their new rescue dog. I also considered it might help some dogs who were struggling, especially if their humans found themselves relating to the problems we experienced. These thoughts gave me the impetus to continue writing down what happened. What I must emphasize, however, is that this is the story of the three dogs concerned and it is not to be interpreted as behaviour advice. What worked and didn't work for them is particular to their journey – another group of dogs would behave in their own ways and their dynamics would be different.

The story begins with our ageing rescued lurcher Ralph, who many by now will be familiar with, having followed his journey since A Dog Like Ralph was published. There is a short summary of his backstory in here, so don't worry if you've not yet become acquainted with him. Ralph's two friends Peggy and Lucy had passed away, leaving huge, gaping holes in all our hearts, and poor Ralph was left alone with his people – us. And Ralph had always preferred dogs to humans.

This is also the story of Nell, the ex-racing greyhound, and Mads, the stray who was abandoned and left to the fate of goodness-knows-what on the streets of a Scottish town. As we came to know them both, it quickly emerged that these two misfit rescue dogs would present us with some problems we'd never experienced with any of the many rescue dogs we'd previously lived with. They were to change our lives, but not always in the ways in which we'd hoped, especially in that first year, or so.

Both dogs arrived with us from worlds alien to me. I have never been able to understand the joy that someone gains from forcing dogs to race, or people who support the racing of dogs and therefore the cruelty which is associated with it. I shall also never understand the abject cruelty of people when they abandon dogs to the lap of the gods.

We can't know for sure what happened in Nell and Mads' lives before they came to us, and I attribute no blame or accusation to any individual whose paths may have crossed with theirs in the past. Any similarity to what actually happened to the dogs is coincidental. I have simply made assumptions based on how they behaved with us because, just like Ralph did more than a decade earlier, they both brought with them troubling idiosyncrasies and ways of being in this complicated world.

Finding Nell and Mads has been a challenging journey. There were times when, even as experienced dog guardians and my being a veterinary nurse, and someone who taught animal behaviour for many years, we wondered what on earth we were doing.

Chapter One

In the Beginning – A Friend for Ralph

It had been nine years since we'd brought Ralph, Peggy, and little Lucy into our family. Huge changes can happen to a household in almost a decade and your dogs live through all those things with you; amid all the highs and the lows, they're there by your side. When you give a home to a rescue dog, often of unknown age and history, you have them only for as long as they have left, not for their whole life as you would do with a puppy. With Peggy, that was only eight and a half years, and Lucy, who we laid to rest just six months after Peggy, we knew for just nine years: the three years she spent with Mum, and then the six she was with us once Mum had passed away.

Conflicting paperwork suggests Ralph's date of birth might be anything from summer 2008 to December 2009, and so, by the time Peggy and Lucy were no longer by his side, he was already an elderly dog who had suddenly found himself alone with his people. He always needed to have another dog around and, likewise, we always like to have other dogs living with us. I suppose that, for me, it's always been a matter of the more dogs I can give a home to in my lifetime, the better, but for Ralph, other dogs have always given him confidence. Dogs are a social species and most of them reap great companionship and comfort from living with other dogs.

And so, Jack Russell cross Lucy and greyhound Peggy left us, and are perhaps watching over us from the great dog sofa in the clouds. Or maybe they're simply resting in the holes we dug in the earth for each of them, somewhere they can be together for eternity under the trees and shrubs which grow above them.

Lucy was a little trooper, and the dog who made me, the lover of medium to big-sized dogs (but, of course, all dogs), understand the joys of living with a small terrier-type. She was our little boss-dog, the dog who the other two looked up (or down) to for reassurance and to keep up to date with what was going on; Lucy didn't miss a single thing that went on in the house.

When Peggy suddenly died, we had just bought a late-1800s cottage to renovate and eventually move into. We decided, even though the renovations would take us a year or two to complete, that we would bury her in the garden there. It was only natural that Lucy would be laid to rest by her side when, six months later, in May 2020, she suddenly passed away too. It took me a long time to get over losing them both. I missed Peggy for her cheekiness, and the way she would give long, warbling barks whenever she was asking for something, and for how gentle she was. Little Lucy I missed for the way, in our private moments, she and I used to dance around the house together, her watching my every move and me encouraging her to follow my every step along the way.

While we searched for another dog, memories of previous dogs and how they came to be with us came to the fore. In March 2011, Lucy had been the first of the trio to arrive in our family, as Mum's dog. Ralph arrived just two months later, and Peggy six weeks after him. Ralph arrived at a time when our previous three dogs – Dillon, Charlie, and Oskar – had all left us in the space of only a year. Those three old dogs had been a group of misfits:

Dillon was a happy-go-lucky, black with some brindle, Labrador cross. His genetic heritage was any number of other breeds, and he was my son Connor's dog, and the kind of canine friend you would wish for your child to grow up loving.

Charlie was a three-legged, liver and white Border collie, aggressive to those he didn't know, and perpetually grumpy to those he did know. Woe betided any of us if we ever tried to do anything with him! Baths were always a nightmare as he growled, snarled, and snapped, while we got all bathing proceedings over with as quickly as possible. No offer of treats or toys to distract him would allay the strong message that Charlie did NOT want a bath under any circumstances.

Charlie had attitude, but we let him off with what was (mostly) aggressive posturing because we knew what awful things he'd been through before being rescued. He'd had a tough time, and his physical scars, when equated against the affectionate dog he was for those who cared about him, reminded us of the dog he could have been. Through the actions of the cruel people who had thrown him from a moving car, however, even with all the love in the world, he was never going to entirely trust any person.

The final dog of the previous group of three to leave us was a tall, handsome, brindle lurcher: the devoted and lovable, yet mixed-up, sometimes dog-aggressive, sometimes food-aggressive, Oskar. He was never sure about other dogs, and we came to understand that the only reason he tolerated Dillon and Charlie was that they both avoided making eye contact with him. They would always look away when he approached them – both cleverly using their subtle, innate actions to allay any escalation in what could easily have resulted in a confrontation.

With Oskar being the last to survive those three dogs, we deliberately gave him those last months without bringing any new dogs into the house. He was old, and his heart was failing, the last thing he needed was another dog in his environment. We really thought we would have more time with him, but even though it was short, I think he enjoyed that period of quiet, just as we enjoyed making it special for him. When eventually we had to let him go, I was sure he'd had enough of the world.

With our home empty, we very quickly found Ralph. He's such a handsome chap who, despite getting on a bit now, is fit for his later years. He loves his walks and having a gentle trot around the garden. He likes some humans and is wary of others. He doesn't dislike other people in that Charlie-collie, 'Don't dare come near me,' kind of way, he just gives people space until he gets to know them.

When we first brought Ralph home, he was lonely, and within a couple of months we made his world complete by bringing our first ever rescued greyhound, Peggy, home from her foster family. In the safe and secure temporary home they'd provided for her, she had been patiently waiting for someone to come along and adopt her. They quickly grew to love her, but they needed to keep a space open in their home to help the next foster dog.

It was when Mum passed away that her mix-of-every-small-breed-possible, but mostly terrier, little rescue dog Lucy, who Mum had loved for three years, came to join us. And thus, Ralph, Peggy, and Lucy became that band of three.

Our dear old Ralph is the epitome of how humans can influence the path of an animal's life. He was badly treated – we don't know for sure how and to what extent, but we know that he somehow escaped that abuse. Just as I'm sure all guardians of rescue dogs do, we tried to piece together what had happened to him before he came to us. We knew he was abandoned on the streets of an English town, left to fend for himself. We were also pretty sure that he was bred to be a hare coursing dog. Hare coursing is now illegal in the UK, and rightly so. Hare coursers breed dogs to chase and kill hares, and the dogs are usually lurchers (greyhound crosses) – dogs who have agility and speed on their side.

Knowing what we know about Ralph from the actions we've observed in him through the years, we believe that he didn't make the grade; that he wasn't very good at chasing hares and was more likely to stand and watch. Whenever there's anything going on with playing fetch and so on, he tends to jump about in a small circle, not knowing what to do with himself. We suspect he did that while other dogs got on with the horrific task of catching and killing the hare. For that lack of killer instinct, it's likely he was punished – and then, ultimately, abandoned. Or perhaps, one day his fright, fight, flight, fawn instinct enabled him to flee – like all dogs with a similar build, he is very fast.

Following his life on the streets, Ralph was collected by a dog warden and taken to a rescue shelter. He was one of many dogs searching for a home, but to no avail, as he was constantly overlooked because of his nervous temperament. He ended up on canine death row in a kennels in England. Eventually, in desperation, a call was put out to no-kill shelters across the UK, in the hope that one of them had a space for him.

And they did.

Our local rescue shelter responded to the call, and he was brought up to Scotland to try to find a home. Within two weeks of Ralph being safe in the shelter, our old boy – mixed-up lurcher Oskar – had passed away, and we were suddenly in a position to give a home to another dog, or two. That was when I saw Ralph's picture on the charity's web page. The rest, I suppose, is history, as the now-elderly boy lies here by my side, while I tap away at my computer.

Ralph's physical scars were on his face, body, and legs, all of them indicating distinct types of injury: a swipe across the face with something sharp; a cigarette burn; damaged dew claws from someone trying to remove them; and multiple scars on his legs. While Ralph's physical scars indicated some of what he went through, like old collie Charlie, the rest was embedded deep in his head; cavernous mental traumas which would never leave him.

What was even worse was Ralph's reaction to being touched on his head. The response became far less prevalent as time went by, but for the first few years after we met him, the fearful recoil he had if anyone approached him, was the saddest thing. The terror he must have been feeling was palpable, and as we tried to comfort him to let him know he was safe, his heart would be racing so hard, it seemed it might burst from his chest. Despite our being sensitive to his needs, that contact with people was something he found difficult to overcome.

Those early months, years even, were incredibly frustrating. I was a veterinary nurse, and I taught animal welfare and behaviour at the local college, I felt that of all people, he should have been able to trust me. But Ralph's fear was so ingrained that we had to take each stage in such tiny steps.

Ultimately, it was me he came to trust first, and we developed a deep bond. We noticed he was better with Connor than he was with Alun, and that he didn't shy away from Connor's hand as he approached him to say hello. Connor is left-handed, and so we all made a conscious effort to approach Ralph with our left hand. It helped, as did Alun lying on the ground and him letting Ralph approach him. Treats helped, but in dogs with a difficult past, they are often nervous of even taking treats from you. Instead, he would nudge the treat from our hand, or glance at the floor to indicate to us that we should put it there for him. It took about six months for his confidence to grow enough for him to take the treats from us. Poor Ralph, it seemed that whatever he had gone through before had severely damaged his confidence.

In time, Ralph began to show the funnier side of his personality, as he danced around reindeer

'Santa Please Stop Here' signs at Christmas (perhaps thinking they were motionless rabbits), and played with the canine friends who came along and who gave him more confidence. In a group of dogs, he always seemed to feel less vulnerable.

And so, after spending those nine years with Peggy, and the final six of those years with both Peggy and Lucy, troubled Ralph was alone again with his humans – us – the ones he eventually finished up with, all of whom loved him dearly. With them gone, he was tolerating the undivided attention, however it was clear that he was desperately missing another being with four legs to nestle down beside, trot along with, play outside with, and, of course, a canine buddy to share the human attention with.

Ralph was also missing the security he'd felt from Peggy and Lucy being around. Ralph likes a peaceful, uncomplicated life, but he was lonely, and bored, often lying on the sofa curled up and sighing to himself. He was clearly grieving and desperately missing the two canine companions he had loved sharing his life with. We were missing Peggy and Lucy too, but this was not about us, it was more about the need to keep Ralph happy, and at the same time, help another dog in need. And so, while the time was fresh since losing them both, the time was also near when we needed to find this elderly fellow a canine friend.

Chapter Two
Enter Nell

We set about scouring rescue websites to look for a dog. It was late-May 2020, and it was tricky searching for a rescue dog in those early, new to the world, Covid times. To protect staff looking after the dogs, shelter rehoming was on hold. Abiding by the guidelines, people were not allowed (and desperately afraid) to be close to one another.

In the days that followed our decision to find another dog, we looked at charity websites that were still showing dogs who would perhaps be available for rehoming under certain circumstances when rules could be followed. We very sadly had to eliminate from our searches many of the dogs we saw. All those rejected or down on their luck, pre-loved, rescue site faces were simply seeking love and a comfortable sofa on which to rest their weary bodies. There were so many dogs we couldn't consider because our search had to primarily consider Ralph's needs. We also very sadly had to eliminate from our search some dogs who were not so pre-loved. Those were dogs who had probably had similar life experiences to Ralph, and we knew that at that point, Ralph needed to be around a dog who had a bit more confidence.

The other dogs we saw, but with a heavy heart had to reject, were just too bold, too young, too aggressive, too bouncy, too big, or too small. There were others who may have been suitable for us, but they'd already been reserved by someone else. It was frustrating that initially there appeared to be no match for us and our dear, gentle Ralph. We had this home available in which a dog would be comfortable, safe, well fed, taken for walks at least twice a day, and above all else, loved, but we needed to make the right choice.

With all the rescues essentially closed and homing having become incredibly complicated, I eventually realized we needed some guidance in finding the dog we could give a home to. If I'm honest, I think I wanted someone else to take the decision out of our hands. We could only take one dog, but the magnitude of emotions I was experiencing through having to choose which one was a huge thing!

I don't know whether I was feeling particularly emotional at that time, having lost Peggy and then Mum's Lucy. Losing Lucy had reminded me of the hurt from six years earlier when Mum had unexpectedly passed away. While you never forget losing someone close to you, you adjust, but then something happens which brings the intensity of all those early bereavement emotions tumbling to the fore. In my case that was losing little Lucy, and the knowledge that Mum had loved her with the whole of her heart.

And then there was Covid, and at that time no

one really knew how bad it was going to get – just that it was like something our world had not seen for a very long time. With everything that was going on, I felt that someone else playing a part in helping us choose a dog absolved us of any responsibility we might have felt towards the others, the ones whose images and sad descriptions we might have been rejecting.

In recent times, some shelters have begun matching humans to dogs, so rather than people who want to adopt marching into a rescue shelter and saying, 'I want that dog,' and the shelter feeling obliged to make that dog fit those people, the people are sometimes matched to the dog. This makes good sense, because shelter staff get to know the dogs in their care, their likes, and dislikes, and with that knowledge comes a sensitivity to an individual dog's needs. Is the dog going to like living with children, other dogs, people who work full time, people who go off hiking every weekend, for instance?

By a family or individual telling the rescue shelter all about their situation, they essentially hand over a hefty part of the choice to them. Seemingly miraculously, they then make a match for the person or family, and the new adoptee comes trotting over to their new family or person, and (in many cases anyway) the dog and their adopter(s) head off into the sunset together.

We all love dogs – husband Alun, son Connor,

who is now grown-up and living and working back at home since the start of Covid, and me – and any dog in need of a home who would be okay with Ralph, would be good with us. It didn't matter about age, or what they looked like, we simply wanted a dog who would like Ralph and who would be gentle with him. When I thought about it, that was the most important thing: gentleness.

And so, having considered many shapes and sizes of dogs, we constantly talked ourselves around in circles and kept returning to rescued ex-racing greyhounds. Ralph had loved Peggy, and she'd had a way of looking out for him. She'd sensed his nervous tendencies and was always gentle around him. We knew we would be lucky to replicate that, but that bond he had with her was subconsciously part of our leaning towards finding another greyhound, or perhaps another lurcher.

Right to the end, Ralph was respectful of Lucy's tiny terrier ways and how she used to flash her little white teeth at him if she didn't approve of anything he was doing, so bringing an unknown terrier into his home right then might have been a little risky. With Lucy, because she'd been Mum's, when Mum passed away we already knew what the feisty little dog was capable of and we also knew that she had a softer side to her. Some terriers can be full-on, leaving tornadoes in their wake, and such an unknown terrier-entity we felt would have been too much for Ralph in his approaching twilight years.

Following our decision being made to steer our search towards another greyhound, I emailed greyhound rescue to see whether they could match a dog to us and our situation. The reply came back quickly. Within an hour! There were four greyhounds ready (assessed, neutered, vaccinated, chipped), so even after my wanting to absolve us from any involvement in a decision, I discovered there was going to be an element of having to choose anyway. My heart sank when I realized this, but in the end, the decision came down to logic and fate.

There were two male dogs and two females. We'd already decided against a male in case Ralph felt a little threatened with having another male around. We'd only ever had him living with Lucy and Peggy and knew that that worked for him – he definitely liked the ladies. So that left two: Mishka and Nell. Two-year-old Mishka apparently disliked non-greyhounds! Some greyhounds are like that, not many, but it happens. Many greyhounds spend their entire racing years never coming across any dogs which don't have their distinct, sleek shape, small greyhound ears, and long pointed muzzles. Their whole life is made up of travelling to races, training, and spending an awful lot of time – often 23 out of every 24 hours, in a kennel. Everything greyhounds do is with other greyhounds – they know and understand greyhound reactions and expressions.

We didn't immediately reject poor greyhound-friendly-but-other-dog-disliking Mishka, though, and I asked her rescuer whether Mishka would even realize Ralph wasn't a real greyhound! I thought we might have been able to have passed him off as an undercover greyhound, after all, he is a tall, sleek hound and people often think he is a greyhound. She thought, however, that yes, it was likely that Mishka probably would realize he was an imposter, especially when we considered Ralph's large, floppy, non-greyhound ears. It seemed her aggression towards any non-greyhounds had been quite severe. Long, heart-rending discussions followed, and we decided it wasn't worth risking upsetting Ralph by taking on a dog with known dog-aggression issues, just in case Mishka really was that bad!

Which left us with Nell.

Ah, Nell. I'd spotted her on the charity's social media pages. She had arrived in rescue just before Covid and was neutered just before lockdown. A couple of weeks later, while out for a run around in an enclosed field, Nell chased a wild rabbit she'd spotted in the distance. As is often their peril, a greyhound has been designed and used by humans to run, and run fast, and as the rabbit safely disappeared to the other side of the fence, Nell decided that said fence was no barrier for a big, strong greyhound. Only it was, and she was never going to make her way under that fence, however hard she tried. By the time her human carers caught up with her, the damage was done. To their horror, at the top of her front left leg, she had an open, lacerated, five-inch wound from where she'd caught herself on some wire mesh.

On hearing that, I had a knot in my belly – our old Peggy had been the clumsiest, most accident-prone dog who had ever been in our lives. Among other misfortunes, she once put her foot down a metal drain and needed stitches for the resulting wound. Was this an omen? I told myself it wasn't, it was just one of those things. Thousands of people have greyhounds, and they get along just fine, without too many mishaps.

With Covid-19 having changed our world, and vets and veterinary nurses not being invincible or immune to such a thing as a brand-new virus which was eagerly transmitting between humans, the veterinary world itself had also changed. Appointments were being reserved for those animals who needed emergency treatment, otherwise, telephone consultations for triage had become the norm.

The wound resulting from Nell's accident was a significant laceration which needed to heal from the inside out, and from the edges to the middle. Lacerations of this kind simply can't be sutured, and this meant she needed frequent dressing and bandage changes. To avoid human to human contact, since the accident the staff at the veterinary surgery had been looking after her in their hospital ward. Poor Nell had been there for six long weeks. Her wounds were still not healed, so it appeared that we would have a delay in getting her home – and thus our lonely Ralph would need to wait for his new companion to arrive.

This accident-prone canine we'd not yet met – Nell – was apparently loving all the attention she was receiving at the surgery. As a veterinary nurse in practice, I used to love it when we had in-patients who were in for a while, and we got to know them well. We'd watch them get better until the time they could be returned to their family and continue their healing in familiar surroundings.

Because nurses who treat humans are people we deal with as individuals in personal times of need, it is often clear to everyone the incredible tasks they perform each day. The work of veterinary nurses is often less visible. Behind the scenes, they are watching over anaesthetized patients and being there for them as they wake, they're inserting and watching over drips, administering injections, taking (and often analyzing) blood samples, helping with imaging such as x-rays and scans, scaling teeth, carrying out minor surgical procedures (under the guidance of a vet), assisting the veterinary surgeon with complex surgeries and neutering, cleaning ears, running their own nurse clinics and so, so much more – and all of this for many different species.

Naturally, the patients are not always cooperative and are often frightened. You can't explain why you're doing what you're doing to them, thus you have to employ a variety of skills to help them relax so that procedures can be over with as quickly as possible. Beyond nursing the array of different animals, veterinary nurses must also be there for their patients' people – at all stages of the animal's life.

When I went into teaching, for many years I missed the hustle and bustle of working in a surgery. There are aspects of it I miss even today, especially the patients and the people who loved them, but also helping with complex surgeries, particularly orthopaedic surgery. I also loved dental scaling – the dirtier the teeth the better, as I knew how much of a difference it would make to the patient's overall health and quality of life. Cleaning out mucky ears I also enjoyed, for the same reasons as dental scaling. Wound care I found fascinating and I loved observing the wonders of nature as it worked away at healing cuts and lacerations – wound care would be especially useful once Nell arrived with us.

And so, beyond having the care of her fosterers and then the veterinary staff, Nell had never been in a proper, loving home. Once she arrived with us it would be her first time living with a family, as she'd not had time before her accident to reach a foster home from the rescue kennel. Given her situation, we reluctantly realized we'd have to hold fire on our excitement until she was ready, and perhaps until Covid restriction-lifting meant she could safely come to be with us. I hoped she would like us and desperately hoped it would be soon. It was strange knowing there was a dog out there who had never met us, and yet her destiny had been determined by a group of people who had known her for only a few short weeks. It already felt as though she were ours, even though all we'd seen of her was a photograph on a social media page — a picture in which she looked terribly unsure of herself.

But then, after thinking we'd need to wait a while for the vets to be happy for her to come to us, Nell's fosterer spoke to them about what was best for Nell, and she was coming to be with us sooner than we'd expected. When the vets and nurses realized she was going to be living with someone who was a qualified veterinary nurse, they said they were delighted to release her from hospitalized care. Remembering, now, that this was still only May 2020 and there was a whole lot of international uncertainty, they'd added that this was on the proviso that we could organize a Covid-safe transference.

We were so happy — Nell would be better off with us — somewhere that she could be taken care of at all hours of the day. I was so very relieved that this would prevent her having to spend more long weeks in the practice. Even though we'd never met her, I'd been awake the couple of nights since we'd agreed to have her, worrying about her being lost and lonely in the practice kennels.

But I needed to worry no more, as Nell was coming home!

Chapter Three

Nell's Adoption Day

Bearing those all-important Covid restrictions in mind, in a local car park we masked humans socially distanced, and like some clandestine package, we moved Nell from her fosterer's car into our own. How often that must happen to dogs even outside of pandemic rules and regulations: destination unknown, and at the utter mercy of the people delivering and receiving them.

The charity allowed us to take her without a home check because we'd previously adopted Peggy from them. Social distancing and home checks were not very compatible in Covid times. Many shelters were holding on to the animals in their care, waiting for a time when the risks might lessen, although at that point there was no sign of that happening. Beyond Covid considerations, many shelters were worried that with people being at home all day, the acquisition of animals might become an impulsive decision. And how prophetic that was of them, as we were to see in the following two years.

Nell was black with a little white on her chest and small flashes of white on her toes – she looked a bit as though she was wearing little white trainer socks. I noticed straight away that she had the sort of black fur which has shades of an amber-brown when the sun catches it. Her face was not as pointed as in some greyhounds (including our old Peggy), and her eyes were watchful, widening to reveal a touch of the white sclera as she looked up at me – confused – who was I? Who was that man beside me?

Nell's body was something else! I couldn't believe the abnormal size of her leg muscles and her rump – she was pretty pumped up and looked akin to a body builder; Peggy's muscles were never that huge.

She panted a lot in the car for the short journey home, she was clearly stressed. This was understandable, given her transference from the car of people she barely knew, to the car of others who were utter strangers. She had arrived with the cumbersome, plastic Elizabethan cone around her head to protect her freshly applied blue bandage from interference by her enthusiastic teeth. Covered in a pawprint design, the bandage shrouded her whole left front leg. The veterinary nurse part of me was bursting to see what was under that bandage – but I had to be patient!

When we got her near to home for the first time, we parked the car, and Connor brought Ralph out to meet her. The warm sun peeked from between the clouds, it was rainy and windy, and we had to do a careful introduction – it had to be Covid-safe so we couldn't go far. Ralph is a nice dog and we'd been told she was dog-friendly too, so we didn't anticipate any problems with them. When he spotted her from a distance, Ralph excitedly wagged his tail in anticipation. He had clearly recognized the familiar shape of a big, black greyhound, and we're sure that for a few moments, from that distance, he thought she was Peggy... perhaps returned after some time away. When they met nose to nose, however, his tail stopped wagging and drooped. The disappointment in him was palpable. I felt my heart breaking for his loss, for the dog standing in front of him, Elizabethan collar framing her face, was not Peggy.

On entering the house, Nell immediately went wild, and began jumping all over the furniture, which was okay for sofas, but her antics also included climbing on sideboards and coffee tables. In the kitchen, she took food from any cupboards she found open and flung it across the tiled floor, and she jumped up at all the work surfaces. She quickly located the dog food cupboards, and then bounced up and down until we fed her. Luckily, her leg bandage and head cone remained intact. Was she going to be the first dog we'd ever lived with who would steal anything we left out on the work surfaces? (This was apart from a misdeed by Peggy once when she stole and ate a whole bar of carob chocolate). Ralph sat back and watched this fiasco unfolding before his eyes, clearly not sure whether this dog was staying or, I'm sure, even whether he wanted her to.

Over the following few days, we all had to learn

that Nell was not Peggy. In anticipation of Nell's arrival, we'd tried to mentally prepare ourselves for this new dog in our lives who was going to, we knew, remind us of Peggy. But there was only ever one Peggy, and there in front of us was this new dog, who was her own dog, with her own personality, her own way of being, and her own needs.

We cried a lot over those first few days. We wept for the loss of Peggy, and for this poor dog who had gone through her own journey and who, through no fault of her own, would never be Peggy. We really had gone into our relationship with Nell knowing this but seeing her standing or lying there looking and being all Peggy-like, it was as though we had Peggy back, only we'd buried her six months earlier. We had never anticipated the strength of feelings we would have in bringing a dog into our home who would remind us so much of Peggy, and who would inadvertently revive the awful loss we had felt when she passed away. Amid all those feelings was the more recent grief we felt at having lost little Lucy. Loving dogs and then losing them does not come easy to anyone who feels that strength of bond with our canine friends.

I'd often wondered how people coped when a dog, say a black Labrador, passed away, and the bereft human companions of the Labrador keenly rushed out to find another black Labrador to join their family. I'd seen it happen many times over the years when working in veterinary practices, and wondered how the new dog would ever fulfil their expectations. I remember one family who deliberately went from a yellow Labrador to a chocolate Labrador when the first one died, to avoid that comparison from happening.

We never, ever, expected Nell to 'replace' Peggy, because we went into the relationship with her with our eyes wide open. And yet, despite the bandage and her (as we came to see) not quite Peggy face, we even called her Peggy by accident a few times. I even called her Lucy once or twice, which I imagine can't be excused at all, given that Lucy's lack of height, little snout, tiny legs, and tiny teeth, meant she was quite far from being anything like a streamlined, black greyhound.

But she was Nell, she was beautiful, and she was actually quite different to Peggy (or Lucy for that matter!). From a distance, you could have been forgiven for thinking she was Peggy, hence Ralph's clear excitement at seeing her for the first time. Close to, however, Nell looks just a bit like Peggy, but more like our lurcher from many years ago – Jack. Peggy's face was more pointed, so much that we used to sometimes call her pointy-faced Peg. Jack was my dear, black lurcher, who saw me through one of the toughest times of my life when I had kidney failure, and I was on dialysis through a tube in my abdomen every day until I was lucky enough to have a transplant. For me, dialysis was only for a year, but for many people it can go on for years, sometimes decades. Jack was my dog, and I was his human, and having him beside me undoubtedly helped me during that awful time. He left us far too soon at the age of just ten.

Normally sweet-natured Ralph spent the first few days grumbling at Nell, and we had to watch them closely to make sure that nothing escalated between them. Nell, however, seemed to sense he was feeling out of sorts and was perhaps a little unnerved at having her around, and she backed off. She gave him the space to sit back and watch her, to see how she was with us, how we were with her, and how everything was going to be. In his Ralph-like way, he yawned at her; taking his cue, she reciprocated with her own yawns. They simultaneously stretched, carefully licking their own lips, each quietly using secret canine signals to tell the other dog, 'It's okay, I'm no threat to you.'

And so, Nell had arrived with us with that huge bandage on her left foreleg and an Elizabethan collar, out of which her forlorn, fed-up face poked. I felt saddened that she had been cooped up at the vets for six weeks. Yes, she'd received six weeks of lots of tender loving care by the vets and nurses in the practice, but just by the very nature of veterinary practices and what dogs hear and see while they're there, and the long times between treatment and short walks, dogs become quite distressed, sometimes resorting to self-trauma. Nell was no exception and had been chewing the end of her tail. It's possible this was something she began doing to comfort herself back in her days as a racing greyhound, as she'd made a bit of a mess of it. Her tail was very long, and even with the cone on to stop her from biting her front leg and the bandage, she could easily reach it. It had probably become a way of her easing the frustration of the confinement of a hospital kennel (or prior to that the racing kennel) and then being restricted by the cone.

I can't imagine how awful it must be to have an itch or a sore and not be able to tend to or scratch it yourself. Often in these circumstances, these problems escalate, resulting in self-trauma to an area of the body they can reach.

Consequently, to prevent further harm to her tail, as well as daily replacements of her leg bandage, we had to keep her tail dressed and wrapped up too. Unfortunately, due to the shape of tails, tail bandages are notorious for flying off when a dog wags their tail. Daily, I would replace the bandage and become obsessive about whether it was still intact. And then my heart would sink as, with fresh bandage in place, she frequently stood in front of me and looked at me playfully, her head shrouded by the plastic cone, wagging her tail so the tail bandage would go flying across the room. Each time, I dutifully applied another one, commandeering husband or son to hold onto her head end, while I carefully wound the bandage around her thin, bony tail. Her tail was extremely thin – and bony. She didn't have much fur on it (which didn't help with the bandaging, as tucking a bit of fur inside the layers of bandage is one method for helping them to stay in place), and you could clearly see the shape of each individual coccygeal vertebra. It looked as though she'd already chewed the end from the tip of it, perhaps about an inch. With all the bandage-changing, it was healing, but I just needed to make sure it stayed covered! I hoped that as time went by her fur would grow back and she'd have the beautiful tail she so deserved.

While Nell's character suggested it wasn't likely she'd been abused by direct acts of cruelty, she had clearly suffered a degree of neglect. Her racing records told us she was four years old, and four years is a huge chunk of a dog's life, about thirty percent of a regular greyhound's lifespan. That's a long time to not have been loved and nurtured; it's a long time for a dog to have had to run for a living. She loved to run, that was clear from the way she raced around the garden, greyhounds do, but surely a dog should be able to run when they want to, and not as the plaything of an industry which sees them as objects to line its pockets?

I feel such rage about greyhound racing and the way people needlessly breed thousands of dogs to heap into a system designed to make money. People may say that it's entertainment and worth the adrenaline rush that those owners, trainers, and gamblers glean from the few minutes the dogs are running, but there is absolutely no justification at all for dog racing. Dogs die, and those who don't die at the hands of the trainers will often arrive in rescue with old injuries, psychological problems, or both. This results in adopters often having to pick up the pieces and provide that additional care they need as they reach their senior years, often more so than the average dog. This is when old racing injuries can become the root of so much pain. I despise the racing industry for what it did to Peggy and what it continues to do to so many dogs.

Nell had won a lot of races, and looking at her mammary glands, they were quite floppy compared to how Peggy was on that under-surface of her body. Had Nell had puppies? If so, that was even more greyhounds who had joined a system that couldn't care less about dogs. Straight away she didn't seem to be the most maternal dog, with her huge muscles and almost aloof attitude, so perhaps that's why she was sent for rehoming. It's possible that even after all her success on the racetrack, she didn't turn out to be so good on the breeding front.

Greyhounds have velveteen eyes, all dogs do, only in greyhounds because of the shape of their eyes, you rarely see the white sclera when they look directly at you, all you see is the chestnut brown velvet of the iris. I think in black dogs this is particularly evident because the brown is the only thing contrasting against the black of their coat, except for the occasional stray white hair or white hairs around their mouth and chin. In Nell, though, she had an expression we had never observed in the eight and a half years we had Peggy, one where she looked up at us and sometimes revealed those whites of her eyes. This was not in what we'd describe as being an aggressive manner in a rabid-Cujo kind of way, more in a playful, 'I'm going to get you to chase me,' sort of expression. That was the expression I had first seen on the day we collected her in the car park. And that look was one we became very familiar with, as it usually preceded an episode of naughtiness.

In hindsight, however, I think that her look on that first day was probably also apprehension. As it was Covid times, we had never got to meet her before she took the rescue shuttle to live with us. That happens a lot these days with dogs being imported from rescues abroad. Viewing a picture and deciding to take a dog on for the rest of their life without first meeting them is a huge undertaking. It requires a lot of hard work once the dog is with you; a dog to keep by your side for the rest of their life.

And so, several weeks in, and there she was in our home – her home – our new dog Nell, with all her idiosyncrasies, and us and Ralph with all ours. For her, the task of getting to know us was far greater than the task we individually had of getting to know her.

Chapter Four

Getting to Know Nell

In those early weeks of her being with us, the cone and the bandage severely inhibited any real attempts for Nell and Ralph to play. How could they play properly when Nell had a plastic cone around her head, a thick bandage from the back of her left elbow to the tips of her toes, a clunky, rubber boot covering said bandage to protect it from the elements and dirt when outside, and a tail bandage weighing the tip of her tail down? With great difficulty, especially when her new companion, lurcher Ralph, was terrified of the thing that was around her head which she kept on accidentally nudging him with each time she walked past, and he was fed up with being hit by her passing bandaged tail.

Lucy had needed to wear a cone a few times over the years for all her terrier scrapes, but there was a huge difference between a small terrier cross in a cone and a big greyhound. Amid all this, Ralph seemed to be concerned about the attention Nell was being given, which in the early weeks had a few times resulted in her whimpering a little when bandages were being changed.

While Nell's leg wounds were slowly granulating, and delicate, fresh pink skin was emerging at the edges and traversing its way across the injuries, they were taking a long time to heal. At one of her twice weekly check-ups, she had apparently squealed the place down. I was outside in the car park waiting for them to bring her out. I hadn't heard her (vet practices often have good soundproofing, for obvious reasons), but I have never seen her more eager to leave anywhere than that day when she dragged the nurse across the car park.

Our own bandaging sessions were thankfully becoming much more relaxed. She was a great patient and taking it all in her stride, only flinching once or twice when I was easing the actual dressing from the open wound, gently making sure the fresh, healing tissue remained intact.

Dogs hate Elizabethan cones; I hate those cones too! Dogs look so sorrowful and clumsy in them. They bump into the furniture, people, and other dogs, but more importantly, they must be incredibly uncomfortable. While Nell still had her leg bandage on, it was easy enough to keep an eye on her and stop her from interfering with it too much, so we would take the cone off when we were able to watch her, and then just put it back on for night-time when we were all sleeping.

Eventually, on the advice of the vet, the bandage was removed so the almost-healed wound could get some air, and we had no choice but for her to wear the cone all the time. We hated putting the collar on her – and from being a relatively lively, happy dog, she descended into despair. Dogs get used to them, sure they do, but I'm certain they don't fully understand why this plastic contraption is stopping them from being able to communicate, eat, or sleep properly. There are now inflatable collars which prevent dogs from turning to bite themselves or reaching down – a bit like an incomplete rubber ring used for swimming, or a neck support some people use when travelling – they're less restrictive, but still look incredibly uncomfortable.

For weeks we had observed this poor dog in the cone, who perhaps thought this was how her life was going to be. We'd had other dogs in the past who'd had to wear them from time to time, but never a brand-new dog who didn't know us before her accident and the resulting wearing of the cone. Was that what she thought? Did she think that she would never be free of it? Did she make any connection in her mind between her gaping wound and the cone?

Using a cone always seems as though we humans are saying, 'We haven't got the time to watch you and check you're not licking your wound, so we'll conveniently (for us anyway) put this collar on and let you go about your business, albeit in a frustratingly restricted manner.' But admittedly, it's hard, and hence like all those in the same situation, and as a last resort, the collar remained on her. We couldn't risk her causing any damage to the by then delicate but slowly healing wound.

As healing tissue finally properly navigated its way across from the edges and inside of the wound, when we were sitting with her, we tried several times to remove the Elizabethan collar, just in case she got it; in case she'd realized that the thing preventing her from freedom was not the collar, but the consequences of what she might have done to her leg whenever she didn't have the collar on. Any damage she did would set her back by days, or even weeks or months. It was a huge wound and there we were, months since the fateful day when she thought she could outsmart a fluffy bunny, and still there was a little way to go.

And, of course, while we could allow a little freedom when she was under the closest observation during the day, at night-time the cone had to go back on, lest we woke up to find an angry looking, weeping wound atop her leg, caused by her incessant, crafty licking during the night.

Alun's such a light sleeper, who wakes up much faster than I do for sounds such as vomiting dogs, dogs standing at the side of the bed to go out for a middle of the night visit to the garden, or dogs who are simply checking up on you while you sleep. This is even if they happen to be standing at my side staring at me to wake up. But even Alun's acute hearing and astute levels of nocturnal consciousness were not sensitive enough to pick up on a canine quietly licking a by-then unbandaged wounded leg. It would be gentle licking which, if sustained over even a few minutes, could be catastrophic to healing. In veterinary practice we would often get people asking whether it would be okay to take the cone off at night. 'No, please don't,' we'd rush to reply, 'as that's precisely when the dog will do most damage to their wound.'

So, the cone remained on at night and also during the day, apart from those few short periods of respite from it when she had our full attention. But there were even times when we did that, and her copybook was blotted; times when out emerged her long greyhound tongue to wrap itself around her wounded leg – and the cone was put straight back on.

And then, three and a half long months after her injury, the wound had completely healed, and she was finally free from the stress of the cone. In the place where the wound had been, there was fresh, shiny skin. It'd been eight weeks since she'd arrived in our lives, and for Nell the initial trauma was six weeks before that.

This eventual freedom for her from the restrictive cone meant that she and Ralph could finally get to know one another properly. In those early cone-free days, she would go up to him several times a day and push her large nose into his face as though she was properly seeing him for the first time. As we came to learn, being in the vicinity of Nell's nose was a bit like being in a wind tunnel – he must have felt that too as she breathed all over him. She'd then sniff his private parts, and he hers... as dogs do. What was most important, however, was that very quickly the fear response Ralph had previously had of her had gone, and they were suddenly able to interact like any other new canine housemates would.

Should we have waited until she was better to bring her home? Absolutely not – for her mental wellbeing, arriving to live with us as soon as she did was the best thing that could have happened to her. By being with us, she had comfy sofas and beds to lie on and constant access to assistance when eating her food and treats and the dreaded cone was getting in her way. She also received bandage changes at the point at which they needed to be done, rather than her having to wait until the ends of clinics or when busy veterinary staff had the time. And, above all else, she was not confined to a cage.

For Ralph, yes of course, he would probably have been better off without her being around through those first eight weeks, but weighing up their two situations, she needed to be with us, and we made it as easy for Ralph as we possibly could. Ralph is a real trooper, and he got through it, which meant we were then able to move forward with them both. We could at last get to know Nell – and she us – without barriers and without her being vulnerable and feeling sore.

Nell began to try to play with Ralph, but Ralph has limited knowledge and enthusiasm for direct play, preferring to stand on the side-lines and watch other dogs play, occasionally taking part with a happy dance and a friendly woof. His not playing leaves the games of fetch solely for the dogs around him, and once that cone was removed, Nell revealed to us what a clever girl she was. I was surprised she knew how to play fetch because Peggy was never that interested, even when little Lucy used to chase a ball and (sometimes when she felt like it) retrieve it. I suppose the game of fetch is a way of making a racing greyhound fit and might be a way some trainers encourage the chase instinct in the dogs, not that these sight hounds tend to need too much encouragement in that department.

Some say that greyhounds often bond more easily with men because, for the most part, greyhound racing is a predominantly male-orientated activity. No matter how they're treated by people, dogs will remain loyal to the bitter end. Kindness can take a long time to break through the walls that a dog who has been badly treated envelopes around themselves. With Nell and me, for some reason we struggled for a while. She clearly very quickly adored both Alun and Connor, but me? There was something holding her back. But I so wanted her to love me.

I missed Peggy's gentle ways so very much, and the funny way in which she used to come over and bark at me when she wanted something. It was not the best behaviour, I know, but we encouraged it, and it just became a part of her. In the times when I was bandaging Nell's leg and tail each day, sometimes more than once a day (especially those blinking flying-across-the-room tail bandages!), Nell was no problem at all. She would see me walking towards her with my pack of bandages and other equipment and would lie down on her side and extend her leg in preparation for whatever I had to do to her wounds. In the end, most of the time I didn't need anyone to hold onto her. Once the wounds were checked, I would wrap them back up again and then give her a 'good girl' treat. I had been nothing but kind and gentle with her, so why did I feel that she didn't actually like me very much?

Because I'd by then retired from teaching, I'd been able to spend every hour with her, and that still being the first wave of Covid meant that, apart from walks, we were all pretty much confined to the house and garden. Even Alun was working from home for a few months. We couldn't even go over to the cottage we were renovating to hopefully move into later that year. When that first lockdown happened, we'd had to down our tools because we couldn't risk going to the house and potentially having an accident on the way there or back, which would further overwhelm a grossly overwhelmed health service. However hard we tried to think of a way around it, we couldn't justify making the journey to and from there, while the medical services were so busy with Covid patients.

Perhaps the thing with Nell was not about me, but more about her and what she had left behind. The dog's ancestor the wolf forms lifelong bonds, and when Nell arrived at the rescue shelter, she had a few companions. In the first few months of her time with us, I sensed Nell was missing someone – whether that someone was canine or human (I doubt any other species, especially not rabbits or cats!) was impossible to tell. She hadn't been in the shelter for long before she had the accident which resulted in her having to stay at the vets while she recovered, so if there was a bond with someone, the bond had been some time before she came to live with us.

We were not really ready for a third dog at that point as we were busy renovating the cottage, however I was curious about her past, and so I scrolled back through the rescued greyhounds to see which ones she had arrived with, to try to imagine whether she could be missing one of them. There were no clues, and there was also nothing I could do about it, because all her companions had by then found their new homes – all headed off on their own new and exciting journeys. And those were high-alert Covid times, so a potential meet-up with other adopted dogs and human strangers was impossible to organize. In the end, all we could do was simply bumble along and make sure she felt as happy and comfortable as we could.

Chapter Five

What on Earth Went Wrong?

Life settled into a reasonable routine. During the first wave of Covid, we managed to keep walking the dogs by going out very early in the morning and very late at night. We hardly saw a soul, except for Ralph's friend Alfie the Yorkshire terrier out on his night-time ambles. While he and his people stayed on the opposite side of the road, we each called across with all our news; there wasn't much, as everyone's life had become very small. I'm sure Ralph and Alfie had no comprehension of why they were suddenly not allowed to meet nose to nose, or to dance and play bow around one another.

And then, the weather was getting significantly warmer, travelling rules had eased, and we could finally go over to our new cottage to continue the work. We'd left it in a state, with ceilings pulled down, the plaster was off the walls, the replacement staircase was unfinished, the upstairs floor was incomplete, there was no heating, the windows had still to be replaced, one window was to be made into a doorway, and there was still an extension to build. Oh, and there was no kitchen or any bathrooms, just one old, yet functioning toilet and an old sink. We had a lot of work to do, but still imagined we could be in by Christmas.

It's strange, isn't it, how that is such an important factor in so many people's house-moving plans? Christmas! It provides a sense of inner joy that we'll all be together amid the festive fun. And so, we set about trying to pick up where we'd left off, and amid all the chaos, we added Ralph and Nell. We'd had this idea, just like the television programmes you see in which people are renovating a house and there's a dog or two happily running around, that we could do the same. Only it wasn't quite like that! Because the house was in such a mess, it was actually quite dangerous for them to be around it, and Ralph hated the banging sounds to the point that he was terrified. And there were a lot of banging noises yet to come.

Disappointed that the dogs weren't able to share in our renovation dream, we decided Connor and I would alternately work at the cottage or stay at home with the dogs, while Alun was the constant foreperson at the cottage. It was incredibly hard work, and I would now tell anyone who was considering a house where complete gutting and renovation was necessary, that it consumes you! That's especially if you're doing the bulk of the work yourselves, as we were. As I write, we've owned the house for more than three years and it is still not properly finished. It is getting there, but I truly think it will be another six months or a year before we've got it how we want it to be. But we're comfortable, and I know there are many millions of people in the world who don't have a roof over their head or even clean water to drink, and that makes me incredibly sad.

I know I've not helped with the speed at which we've done the house, as there are some things I felt needed to be done very quickly – like sorting out the garden and planting trees. Most people have probably by now heard the adage, 'The best time to plant a tree was twenty years ago, the next best time is now,' and I was desperate that we used the space wisely, creating an orchard and a garden that would be welcoming to wildlife. We've so far planted more than eighty trees, three hedges, and so many shrubs and flowers I couldn't count them. But we've seen such a difference.

When we arrived, the ground was incredibly waterlogged, and Alun spent weeks creating proper drainage. Where there's a large, complex burrow, we've created a safe haven to protect the rabbits from the dogs. Along with the established large trees and hedgerow, the new trees and hedges are already supporting birds, squirrels, and insects, and in the years to come there will hopefully be fruit for one and all.

It became a bit of a joke with some friends that whenever they asked us how we were getting on with the house renovations, we would respond with a quick change of subject and tell them instead how the garden was coming along. I think we were in denial at the sheer amount of work we had to do to make the house into a home, and spending time outside gave us the peace we craved.

One memorable afternoon, we had pulled down the old ceiling in what was to become the dining room. At lunch time, the sun was shining outside and so we stayed out there for the rest of the day, building the boundaries for the new compost heap. I think without doing things like that we would have gone quite mad, especially with one another, as we both had our own way of doing things and both thought our way was better. Outside, we could forget the magnitude of what we still had to do inside.

Having arrived with us mid-lockdown, and then having the disruption of us all coming and going between the house and the cottage, along with still not having a completely healed leg, must have been mentally traumatic for Nell. I suppose as I write that, I'm trying to figure out what it was that provoked what transpired with her later that summer…

It was morning time, and the sun was shining brightly through the bedroom window. We'd already taken Ralph and Nell for their first walk of the day, and I was in the bedroom getting ready to go out to the garden store for my first 'trip out' since the start of Covid. Nell had followed me upstairs. I called her up onto the bed and she lay down beside me. She'd previously stood or lay down on the bed many times just like that while I'd been getting dressed, and I continued brushing my hair. Once

I'd finished, I stood up, and at the same time, Nell also stood. She was looking at me in what I thought was a normal way, there was no sign of her being unhappy with me, so I put my face close to hers to talk to her and, whoa, she snapped at me – right in my face.

I was stupid, I know, and I should have known better, because putting your face close to a dog's face like that can be perceived by the dog as being threatening. It really was a stupid, stupid thing for me to do. But there had never been any sign that she wasn't comfortable with closeness. When it happened, I instinctively recoiled from her and immediately burst into tears!

My instant thought was a deep loss for Peggy – dear, gentle old Peggy – and all I could think of was that I'd 'replaced' her with a monster. I missed Peggy so much. On some very rudimentary level, did Nell sense that my heart was still with Peggy? Although Lucy had passed away more recently than Peggy, and the loss was just as intense, the terrier ways she had had because of her mixed heritage meant that Nell did not remind me of her at all. With little Lucy I didn't have that constant reminder in the shape and size of a big, black greyhound.

It seemed I had inadvertently found us one of the very few greyhounds who have aggression problems. They're normally such gentle, easy-going, calm, friendly dogs, but who's to know what goes on in a dog's life – where they've been, who or what might have hurt them? It's the same with people's lives – if we had a window into someone's life and we could see what some people must endure day on day, we'd probably be astounded and perhaps more understanding in how we are with others. For the most part, people can tell you what's wrong; with rescue dogs, we have no clue, and we must unravel those problems layer by layer.

Peggy had been an easy dog to be around, and an absolute joy. I think despite her track days, she had been treated well by whoever she had been with before and therefore had less baggage, but with Nell, who could tell? She couldn't tell us; we could only assume that there were some gremlins in her past that she was having difficulty overcoming.

I was incredibly relieved that there was no follow-through from her after she snapped at me – she didn't lunge forward or try to bite me properly. I think it was just an 'Enough, that's too close, don't come near me,' warning. While tears of sadness ran down my face, I immediately told her to get off the bed and encouraged her to follow me downstairs. I was in shock, but knew I needed to remove us both from the situation that had just happened. She followed me as though she would follow me if I was taking her out for a walk; any reaction to what had just happened between us was completely absent. It puzzled me! Was there any comprehension from her at all about what had just gone on?

Meanwhile, alarm bells of everything I've ever known about unprovoked aggression in dogs tumbled through my head. But then, I did provoke her, didn't I? I invaded her space!

I wondered in the months that followed whether what happened that day, and the events that came afterwards, were expressions of resentment towards me because I had been the one to take care of her wounds. It was baffling, though, because she had been perfectly behaved when I was changing her bandages and treating her leg and tail wounds. Was it that in her mixed-up mind, she thought I was responsible for her leg injury and tail mutilation?

I'd never before lived with a dog who had tried to bite me – yes, there had been Charlie the three-legged collie, but he was like that with most people, and with us it was only if ever we were trying to do anything with him for his own sake (like bathing, clipping nails). The rest of the time, Charlie was like a cuddly teddy bear. With him, you could predict it, there was ALWAYS a Charlie-reason-why, and we made sure he was never a danger to anyone.

With old Oskar the brindle lurcher, too, it was always other dogs and always to do with resource possession, i.e., food, a toy etc., and if he wanted something, he was going to get it by whatever means, even if it meant threatening to bite his canine housemates. Oskar never once threatened to bite us, and we made sure he didn't bite Jack, Dillon, or Charlie by leaving him in our bedroom when we weren't there, and making sure resources were never an issue when we were. Toys in the house were banned and we had individual play with him – the others would happily play together. But with Nell, the trigger seemed to be much more subtle. What did I do? Did I remind her of someone who had hurt her? Or was it, indeed, my involvement with the regular bandage changes and the soreness that had inevitably sometimes caused her?

As I mentioned, it's well known that greyhounds can sometimes be a bit indifferent towards women and are known to bond much easier with men – female greyhounds are often particularly fond of their male guardians. Peggy was never like that, and I'd like to think she liked me as much as she liked Alun and Connor. But perhaps with Nell, it was something as simple as preferring men to women, or, again, perhaps she had been hurt by someone who was like me.

It was difficult to be around a dog who had shown aggressive tendencies towards one of us. If it had been other people and a specific type of person, then it would have been something we could have easily controlled by avoidance of the situations which provoked the aggressive reaction, but we lived with her – I was around her every day.

It's curious that the dog who went into rescue at the same time as her also had aggression problems – I have often wondered whether they were related. Perhaps there was some trigger in both their lives which had made them that way? She has an old scar on the back of her neck, for example, which is perhaps from a fight with another dog. It's one of the classic places for such injuries. Or perhaps it came down to the whole nature versus nurture thing, and it was something 'in' her – something genetic?

Perhaps it was that her mother experienced more maternal stress during pregnancy than even the average racing greyhound does, for it's now widely accepted that maternal stress during pregnancy can cause emotional problems in the offspring. Pregnancy in a kennel block would definitely cause huge levels of stress to the dam. But none of this explained why whatever happened had changed into aggression towards people.

I thought it was only me she was struggling with, but then over the coming months it happened again, and not just with me! After what had happened that day, we knew not to go near her for 'face-hugs' (not advisable in any dog, but some dogs – such as Ralph – seem to enjoy that closeness). It still happened more with me than with Alun and Connor, but in a few months we had about ten incidents – most were with me, but then I was with her more often than anyone else.

I was in despair, as I had never before had a dog who didn't appear to like me. I'm one of those sometimes antisocial 'prefer dogs to people' people. How could a dog not seem to like me? I'd spent decades working with dogs and knew how to be around them to minimize stress, even in difficult situations. I had given the likes of strong German shepherds injections, giant breeds such as Saint Bernards ear drops, tiny Chihuahuas drops in their eyes, and put hundreds of dogs onto intravenous infusions. I had also taught animal behaviour for years. Above all this, we as a family knew how to interact with dogs, and we'd given her everything she needed. So what was wrong?

She snapped a few times at Ralph, and you could tell from his reaction that he was incredibly worried by her actions. After that, if they were lying on the sofa together, we'd put a cushion between them. That summer and autumn, on no occasion with us or Ralph was there any follow through with further aggression – she snapped, never made contact, and then it was over. Afterwards, it was almost as though she was oblivious to what had just happened – it was like it was something we were experiencing, she would see us backing off, however she had no idea that she had been the one to make us do that.

Renovations at the cottage were making us all very tired, yet we made sure Ralph and Nell had little deviation from their routine – they were fed and walked at the usual times and had regular playtimes. The rest of the time, one of us was there with them, always making sure they were okay. While they probably sensed our fatigue, they were protected from all that stress, all the dust, banging and everything else that was going on over at the cottage, so we were sure it was nothing to do with that.

We looked for clues in Nell's behaviour, in how we were acting with her, and how we were with Ralph, but there was nothing. Very gradually, as we mentally sifted through everything we knew about what was happening with her, we realized there actually was a key factor which, apart from that first incident (which was because of my own stupidity), connected all of the other incidents.

Chapter Six

Renovations and a Move

Our house back then was in suburbia with countryside on our doorstep, which for the most part, was inaccessible (despite there being a 'right to roam' law in Scotland), so we mostly walked the cycle routes. As Covid rules eased, when out walking, we went back to pre-Covid restriction times of seeing many dogs of all shapes and sizes.

Dog-loving Ralph was in his element as he was at last able to nuzzle nose to nose his best friends. But Nell had never been a town dog, and it must have been a huge shock for her to have moved from a life of kennels and racing, through all she went through with her leg injury, and then finding herself surrounded by houses. Not only lots of houses, but all the pampered, domesticated animals those houses contained. It was as though dogs and cats were oozing from the brickwork of all the buildings – some old friends of Ralph's, and many new animals acquired as companions during lockdown.

This sudden contact with other dogs was overwhelming for Nell, and this was perhaps part of her being unsettled – she'd come from a life on the tracks where non-track time was spent training for the tracks or spending long hours enclosed in a kennel. She'd not known dogs other than greyhounds, and that scar on the back of her neck suggested she'd not necessarily always got on with them. If a little clumsy at times, Ralph was a gentle dog, so we were sure there was little stress involved in her being around him but, still, it seemed there was something deeper going on with her. We continued to be careful with her, tried to minimize her stress on walks, and got on with our lives.

The cottage was taking an incredible amount of time; I went out and optimistically bought paint, perhaps thinking that if it was there ready for me to use, it would make the whole thing happen more quickly. It was not to be, and while Alun and Connor got on with making the inside of the house habitable, I neatly lined up my paint pots and frequently looked longingly at them, imagining the day when I could start filling the house with an array of beautiful colours.

In the meantime, we struggled against the increasingly adverse weather conditions to put up fences and plant hedges, and when the weather did allow, I got on with filling holes in between the stones of the outside walls of the cottage and then painstakingly painted all the exterior walls.

One of our hedge planting experiences was on a Friday night in the dark, and in the worst downpour we'd seen for a long time. Afterwards, we were soaked through, but felt incredibly happy that we'd got the plants in the ground. The hedge is now almost three times the size it was when we planted it and it's filling out; in a couple of years, it will provide a decent habitat for small birds. It was those aspects of moving that kept me feeling optimistic when it seemed as though we were making such little progress on the inside of the house.

While we got on with the cottage and looked after the dogs in shifts back at the house, it became apparent that apart from not liking strange dogs so much, Nell had also clearly not been around cats before. Peggy had been incredibly anti-cat too, but Peggy was about eight kilogrammes lighter than big, strong, muscular Nell, so any sign of a cat rushing by was never as dramatic with her as it was with Nell. Luckily with Nell, however, we quickly discovered she was food orientated, so rewarding her for ignoring cats became very effective. You just had to spot the cat first, or else that hound-drive took over and along the street we'd be pulled, with all her greyhound might.

As summer turned to autumn, and gold and amber leaves were hanging from the trees as they progressed towards their winter dormancy, Nell's fur began to fall out of her hind legs. We'd got ourselves a neurotic greyhound who also appeared to have seasonal baldness, or bald thigh syndrome, which is relatively common in greyhounds. It's thought it could be hormonal due to the high demands imposed upon their bodies. It's also thought it could be due to poor welfare or a poor diet. When spring the next year came along, the hair grew back again, but I supposed that forever she'd be walking around in the colder months with a bald behind. Hers was not bad compared to some greyhounds I'd met, but it was quite obvious, and something which only added to the complexity of our mixed-up dog.

Many dogs who were acquired during the several lockdowns will have missed out on the socialization they should have received in their new lives, as people had to distance themselves from others and, consequently, others' dogs. The breeding and sale of puppies boomed as some made mid-Covid decisions to make their lives or walks more interesting, and some breeders opportunistically took advantage of this, swamping the dog market with thousands upon thousands of puppies.

While rescue organizations had tried to do the right thing by closing their doors to keep everyone safe, young dogs began appearing everywhere we went. That made me sad, because however much we may love to see a cute, playful puppy, and however much they give us that warm glow inside, they have complex needs and should never be a spontaneous decision. I feared that post-Covid many would end up in shelters; the novelty worn off, and dogs' needs greatly underestimated.

And so, while all Nell's problems came tumbling out, we continued to acknowledge that, apart from that first time with me when she had been fully alert, whenever Nell snapped at us there was never any follow-through, i.e., she would never go on to bite. It was always a warning snap, which never made contact with our skin.

As time passed, the snapping became less frequent, however we noticed two key things, the first being that it only happened whenever we were unexpectedly around her head end. The second key factor that dawned on us was that, apart from that first event, every other time it happened, it was when she was in that resting zone between being awake and asleep, or vice versa. With Ralph, too, from time to time, if he got too close to her or shuffled about when they were both resting and she was almost asleep or almost awake, then she would snap at him. At this, he would quickly jump off the sofa. By November 2020, which was six months after she'd arrived in our lives, we continued to acknowledge that it was always a single snap in the air, and after she'd done it, she still looked at us as though nothing had happened.

Needing to spend far more time at the house, we decided to get it as habitable as possible and just move there. We'd reached a point whereby our money was dwindling and there was no more room on our old mortgage to pay for the work we needed to do on the cottage. We decided to put the house on the market so we could release the equity we had left so we could pay back the money for the purchase of the cottage and fund the rest of the repairs on it. We thought it would take several months to sell the house, giving us time to prepare our new abode for a peaceful arrival. Only it didn't – it sold within a few days of being on the market and so we needed to plough on at the cottage and complete a bathroom, somewhere to cook, at least two bedrooms, and somewhere to sit.

Those two months between selling and moving, and then the actual move, became the most stressful house move we'd ever made. We were downsizing but then making the cottage bigger so it would be the same size as the previous house, but we wouldn't owe anyone anything. It was a dream, but it was a dream that was difficult to achieve, and on those cold early December days after we'd moved to the cottage, I wondered what on earth we'd done!

I can remember sitting, staring into the distance after walking the dogs one morning, and Alun asking what he could do to help. I had my coat on my lap and I said, 'I just need somewhere to hang my coat,' and let out a huge sigh. And so, we set about building a cloak room just inside the hall and that cleared the coats from all the corners of the cottage where they'd been scattered. It was a good, functional start to our new lives. I felt pathetic about being so needy, but I was exhausted – as we all were.

Shortly after that, I realized I had spoken too soon about our problem with Nell always being her making single snaps in the air. It was a week or so before Christmas and Nell gave her most fearsome snap ever. I couldn't bear to think that the problem was escalating. She was lying next to me, and I innocently leaned across her to pick up my laptop from the coffee table which was at her end of the sofa. I thought she was awake, but perhaps, as we'd started to acknowledge, she was in the throes of that sleep-awake/awake-asleep phase. I knew afterwards that I shouldn't have been so complacent; I should have checked she was properly awake, or not been so lazy and stood up to go and get the laptop. That time, she did three consecutive snaps in the air, and because I was leaning over her, my face was quite close to hers – luckily, my reactions were very fast. I found myself trembling with fear. We were all in the room and, as I recoiled, we all shouted, 'No, Nell!'

As before, there wasn't any snarling, no baring of the teeth, just the three snaps. But nevertheless, that day it was terrifying. I truly believed in those early times that she could not have lived with children, with the ways in which they have such unpredictable movements.

In the weeks that followed, while desperately wondering what to do, we became ever more careful around her. She had a problem – we had a problem! Were we being naive in thinking we could heal her? What if one of us was injured? I spoke to behaviourist friends – they agreed we were doing all we could, but when did our being careful become reckless?

Despite us still having heaps and heaps to do in the house, Christmas time was arriving fast, and we optimistically placed a Christmas tree in one of the front windows and put lights along the garden fence. It was a toned-down version of what we'd normally have done, but it was Christmassy, and we knew we needed to make an effort – doing it forced us to relax for a while.

That was the first Covid Christmas, and rules dictated everyone must have a quiet time; while a little mixing between households was allowed, it was being actively discouraged. The only person we mixed with was Mark, my brother, who was classed as our 'extended household' as he lives alone. Like me, he was shielding, only with him it was because he was on kidney dialysis, rather than in my case because of my transplant medications. He was with us for Christmas Day and Boxing Day, before he had to go back home to attend the hospital for dialysis; so many years, so many Christmases that dialysis had to be a factor in everything he did. Three times a week, every week for so much of his life. I truly hoped that the new year would be the one in which he would be lucky enough to receive a transplant.

Resting, it seemed, had a positive effect on Nell. We were being much more careful around her, so perhaps the resting and our awareness were combining to make her less stressed. Was it stress? I wished she could tell us what was up with her. Perhaps the injuries she sustained, coming to live with us, having all the backwards and forwards during the major renovations of the cottage, and then moving, had all contributed to her feeling out of sorts. Perhaps she was over-tired and therefore got a shock and was overly grumpy each time she was woken suddenly. But that didn't explain the first incident when she was standing on the bed, and clearly very wide awake (but I insist that that was my fault!).

And so, there we were, the bells had chimed across the world, and we'd entered another new year, one which, globally, people were hoping would be better than the last. With Nell, we'd trodden carefully, each of us being aware that she wasn't keen on close face contact, we must not disturb her when she wasn't quite awake (accidentally or otherwise), and that we mustn't ever, ever lean across her. It was like a list of warnings from the film *Gremlins*: don't feed after midnight, never expose to bright lights... It was hard, however, because our natural instincts were for us to treat her in the same way we treated Ralph, and all the other dogs who had been before. Ah, except Charlie, of course!

For Ralph, it was more difficult, because he couldn't be a part of our human family conferences on how we were to interact with Nell. Instead, he had to learn from his mistakes, by watching her behaviour and responding to what she was doing in his gentle Ralph way – by not snapping back at her, and simply retreating from the situation.

We were helping them as much as we could, for example if they were both lying on the sofa together, then we continued to place a cushion between them to prevent him from accidentally touching her when she was in that danger zone of being on the verge of waking or sleeping. But it was difficult, not least because we had wanted to find Ralph a friend and at the same time, give a homeless dog a home.

We had never anticipated any problems. They were problematic to the extent that I was sure I couldn't trust leaving Nell and Ralph home alone together. Because of Covid, they had always had someone home with them. We were so busy working in the house that until we stopped for a little while over that Christmas, we realized that seven months had passed since Nell came into our lives and she and Ralph had never been alone. This had never happened before with any of our previous groups of dogs – or dogs and cats when we used to have cats too. We'd always needed for previous dogs to have some home alone time and, for the most part (except resource-possessive Oskar, our old brindle lurcher), they'd been fine.

We needed to address the problem as soon as possible – and the best way was going to be in the same way we would treat a dog with separation anxiety – little by little, accustoming the dogs to being home alone. That began with them simply being in the house on their own for a few minutes and then working our way up to a couple of hours. We also left without making a fuss and returned in the same manner. We made sure there were no places where they could lie down side by side – all beds and chairs were separated from one another, and one end of each sofa had cushions removed so that only one dog would lie down on the comfortable end. And they were fine – each time we came home, they would both greet us at the door wagging their tails.

And then, as suddenly as Nell's behaviour had begun, by the end of January 2021, it actually seemed to have stopped! I've always been prone to speaking too soon and didn't want to do that, so, very tentatively, and quietly, I whispered to the others, 'It's been more than a month since Nell has snapped at any of us!' There seemed to be something different, something better about her (or even our) dynamic.

Perhaps we had become more respectful of how she was feeling and more respectful of giving her space, or perhaps she had become more tolerant of us and our strange human (and Ralphie) ways, but the dog we had longed for was suddenly in our midst.

By the end of February, Nell had truly begun to reveal some of her more conventional greyhound quirks, such as lying on her back when she was resting, sticking her nose right up to things to examine them, and being alert to everything going on around her – she was a sight hound, after all.

There must have been something up with her during those few months, but we never got to the bottom of it. Pain was something we considered, but we were sure that wasn't what was wrong with her, because I had checked legs, ears, mouth, belly, and all the other places someone might think could be causing her pain. And anyone who lives with a greyhound will tell you that greyhounds tend to let you know when they are sore.

She did have a bit of an ear infection at one point, but it was so mild that a few days of ear drops sorted her out. And she loved having the ear drops in and me massaging her ears. We never, ever gave her face hugs – some dogs simply don't like that closeness. Ralph always loved the security of you smothering him with love and wrapping yourself around him, but we knew that would never be Nell's thing. She licked us from time to time (and especially loved her human dad's hairy grey beard or stubble), but any contact like that was always on her terms and with her initiating it – and, quite naturally, for everyone's safety, we discouraged it by distracting her with toys.

Winter was drawing to a close, and warmer days gave us much more opportunity to use the big garden (as opposed to the regular-sized one), which had through the winter become a bit of a quagmire. When we had moved in, we'd had to create the regular sized garden by fencing behind the house because, timewise, at that point it would have been impossible for us to have fenced the whole perimeter of the property. It had worked though, as it protected the dogs from the dangers in the bigger garden, and at that time there were many.

There are two derelict 1800s buildings on that part of the property, in which generations of locals must have been dumping waste. In the end, it took us four skips to sort out the rubbish – and that was with recycling whatever materials we could along the way. Much of that rubbish was glass and when we began digging, we found other pockets of glass disposal all over the garden. Additionally, once we did have the perimeter fenced, we couldn't let the dogs in until we'd cleared the vicious, thorny briars that would have ripped both dogs' delicate skin.

When the drains began working, the rubbish had gone, and we had cleared the space of old briars, it was heart-warming to see Nell and Ralph running around and using the whole garden – the garden space had been the reason we'd bought the cottage.

As I mentioned before, we didn't teach Nell how to play fetch, she already knew how to play it when she arrived, and she's extremely good at it! One day in February 2021, we had a clue to what the person who taught her fetch might have looked like. We were playing games with her and Ralph in the back garden and Connor threw the ball into the distance. While all this was going on, my parents-in-law arrived, and we let them in through the garden gate. When Connor threw the ball again, on her return, Nell promptly took the ball and dropped it at my father-in-law's feet, instead of taking it back to Connor.

She was incredibly excited to see Robin, who, because of Covid restrictions, she had only ever seen through windows when we dropped by their back garden on our walks. She'd never until then seen him in that setting, and until that point had never seemed to associate the game with anyone other than the three of us who are her guardians. She was enthusiastically encouraging him to throw the ball for her – it was as though she knew him well and he was her long-lost 'fetch' buddy. She suddenly became utterly oblivious to the rest of us.

My father-in-law walks with a stick, has pure white hair, and on that day was wearing a red baseball cap. I became, then, convinced that whoever she was missing was human, and it could have been that the person resembled my father-in-law. She didn't ever do it again, although she would become excited when he and Alun's Mum came to visit. I think that somewhere in her canine understanding she must have separated the man in the red cap from the person who taught her to play. But, of course, playing fetch is a form of exercise and the game was possibly (probably... given that the person concerned relinquished her to rescue) more to do with keeping her fit, than any great desire to bond. Dogs are forgiving, and I've seen the most awfully treated dogs give their devotion to the perpetrator of their abuse. A bit, I suppose, like Stockholm Syndrome.

In some ways, it made me feel better that it was possible the missing was to do with people – we could continue trying to fulfil that role for her. Had she been missing another dog (and she may still have been because what we were thinking was complete speculation), that would have been more difficult to help her with.

When Ralph arrived with us, he had the most awful diarrhoea. As his stress levels reduced over time, so did his digestive problems. Nell's diarrhoea was, however, unbelievably persistent. We tried so many different light diets, and eventually found one that suited her tummy. Never, though, through all those months, did she ever go to the toilet in the house, even when she must have been desperate. Every dog we'd ever brought to live with us had at some point had a toilet accident, but never Nell. Not a single tinkle on the rug! We were amazed at how clean she was. She had never been in a home – had it perhaps been the time when she was hospitalized at the veterinary surgery which had given her some idea about not going to the toilet inside? I think it must have been that. She would have got into a routine of being taken outside by the nurses. I wouldn't, however, recommend a dog injuring themselves by chasing a bunny under a wire fence, and subsequently spending all that time in the veterinary clinic, as a way of learning how to not toilet in the house!

As the months went by, Nell stopped sighing so much. She didn't seem to be searching any more – perhaps she'd given up hope of seeing whoever she was missing. I suppose she simply embedded herself into our routines and our family's ways. At the time she arrived, Ralph was lonely, and I suppose these two lost souls were just forced into a situation created by us humans. She and Ralph gradually grew to be affectionate towards one another, but he was old, and she was sometimes a bit boisterous with him. Gradually, however, they played nicely together. She'd race around the garden, while he'd try to catch her – mostly unsuccessfully unless he took a shortcut between the trees. In their quiet times, they began to lie together on the sofa and rest their heads on each other's backs (at last with no need for a cushion to separate them).

As the fullness of spring came along, we were glad we'd invested the time we had into nurturing our relationship with Nell. There had never been any thought of giving up on her, but it was hard, and there were times when we thought she would never be safe to be around – to the extent that we wondered if we would ever overcome the terrible situation in which we'd all found ourselves. But then, as the months passed, we realized we were only needing to invest the same amount of caution into our relationship with her as we would any dog. These great outcomes came from rewards-based training, something to which she was incredibly responsive.

Nell was okay, and it had taken time, but together we had climbed the hugest emotional hurdles for her to be relaxed around us – and us with her.

Chapter Seven

Living in the Country: Rabbits, Rodents, Feathered Friends... and Dogs and Cats

Wild animals tend to remain well hidden in the winter months and spring was arriving with all its new life. Only we'd quite accidentally bought a house which had a rabbit warren in the garden. It's a complex network of tunnels beside two huge Douglas pine trees, flanked on the other side by a multi-trunked sycamore – a tree which must be about two hundred years old – and an old oak tree.

We had a greyhound and a lurcher, both of whom had previously been used in one way or another to chase rabbits or hares, albeit in Nell's case, a mechanical hare. To be fair to us, when we viewed the house, it was August-time, and the ground at the back had been covered in nettles – thousands upon thousands of them. There was no way of knowing that there were rabbits living there. I'm sure even the guy selling the cottage, who had before selling it to us rented it out to tenants for decades, wouldn't have known of the rabbits' des-res garden accommodation.

It was only as December had rolled in and the nettles had properly died down, that we saw these carefully engineered tunnels emerging. We're all nature-loving vegans, so they were perfectly safe from the gun and a butcher's knife, but we were worried they would not be quite so safe from the jaws of two dogs — especially the big, muscular, astutely vigilant Nell. But a colony of rabbits was not necessarily going to be our only animal-related predicament in our new abode.

We were in a new area. We had moved the dogs from a place in which Ralph had lived for seven or more years, and it was the only house Nell had ever known. With a new neighbourhood comes new dogs, new streets to walk along, a completely new world of smells to explore. While Nell despised the dogs in the new locality even more than she'd despised the ones who lived near our last house, Ralph slipped into what appeared to be a canine depression. He lay on the sofa, quiet and not interacting, he sighed a lot, and he went off his food. He hated his new walks, scurrying along the streets as quickly as possible and not wanting to stop and sniff the trees, walls, and lampposts. This was not our Ralph, our happy-go-lucky, dog-loving Ralph. He missed his old walks and Buster, Chester, Alfie, and Dexter — all the little dog buddies he'd gathered along the way. In trying to do something good for the dogs by finding them a house with a garden in which they could have a really good run around, we'd inadvertently made them miserable.

But dogs are very adaptable, and a few months in, Ralph was strutting his stuff around the streets, raising his leg against all lampposts, trees, and any other interesting vertical surfaces he could find. Nell, meanwhile, had ditched any real interest in the local canines, and instead located the addresses of all the feline citizens. She was spending her walks vigilantly scrutinizing their whereabouts.

The bigger garden was eventually nicknamed with the acronym BG. This was the secret name we would use when we didn't want the dogs to know we were talking about that garden. As dogs do, like when you spell out the word 'W-A-L-K' to prevent dogs from getting excited too soon when a walk is about to happen, the dogs came to know 'the BG' and any mention of it induced similar reactions to mentions of the 'W' word.

We had deliberately kept the fence that we'd erected to separate the two gardens. This was so that canine nocturnal visits outside would be possible without said canines heading off for a wander, chasing bunnies, or whatever dogs do as delaying tactics when you're standing shivering by the back door in the middle of the night, waiting patiently for them to come back in.

The rabbit warren is luckily in the BG, and therefore we were able to go and check the area for grazing rabbits each time before letting the dogs run riot. And, for the most part, this worked. When Nell came close to catching a rabbit we'd not spotted on our check, however, we realized we'd have to up the ante in our efforts to protect our long-eared, little mop-tailed friends.

And then, we had a great idea! We hadn't wanted to erect a fence as it would have blocked off another part of the garden, but what about all the branches and sticks lying around from the ash trees? In even the mildest winds, it seemed that ash trees cast branches, and because when we arrived there was so much garden obscured by nettles, we didn't find these branches until everything died down.

We have eight large ash trees in the garden, resulting in many branches. Aha, we thought, we could build a barricade of branches around the rabbit warren, thus, the rabbits could still get in, but it would serve as a barrier to large dogs; simultaneously, it would look more natural than a fence. Perfect! And so, we enthusiastically gathered sticks and built our barricades. We've since discovered this is an official, horticultural structure known as a 'dead hedge,' and we'd accidentally stumbled upon something which provides a habitat for any number of small creatures. The creatures benefiting are mostly of the entomological kind but also, for us, it became the start of the walls to the des-res of our local lagomorphs.

And it helped. Nell's not one to apply too much logic to anything (not that I'm suggesting greyhounds aren't very clever, but they're not considered too favourably on the canine intelligence scale), and such a barrier was enough to hold her back from following the rabbits to their home. The dead hedge immediately offered a sanctuary to any she might have tried to catch, and we've since added to it with any prunings or branches cast from the trees.

That predator-prey race is quite something, and rabbits have developed ways of ducking and diving to avoid being captured by potential predators, just as those predators developed astute senses to spot the potential prey in the first place. Ralph, well despite his own astute senses, he just wasn't too bothered about the rabbits, except to be interested in Nell's interest in them.

Living in the town, we'd fed many species of garden bird and asked the people who bought the house to continue with that routine. We'd also seen buzzards flying over, sometimes alone, sometimes in groups of three or four, and the magnificent dawn and dusk flights of a large group of jackdaws often coincided with our dog walks.

Quite early on in our renovations of the cottage, we had regular visits from a robin. When we hired a digger, as Alun was moving from place-to-place shifting soil to insert new drains, the robin would go and catch a ride on the bucket. The little bird also found his way into the digger's cab a couple of times. They're cheeky, those robins, often quite fearless – and also extremely bossy, but they're nice to have around. Other than him and a few jackdaws, when we began the cottage renovations, there were not many birds. But putting out food and creating natural habitats draws birds into a garden, and once we did that, they came in their droves.

Rooks, blue tits, coal tits, great tits, wrens, starlings, blackbirds, chaffinches, sparrows, yellowhammers, thrushes, collared doves, wood pigeons, the jackdaws brought along more jackdaws, and gliding across the skies, were buzzards and red kites. The nut feeder attracted a woodpecker, a treecreeper, and a nuthatch, the dandelion 'clocks' attracted goldfinches and, of course, the little bossy robin stuck around.

Birds give such immense pleasure, perhaps because they represent a freedom little known to us humans. We can sit back and watch them as they go about their business, as they mix in with other avian species with little malice towards one another. We can hope that by providing habitats and feeding them, we are somehow helping them to survive. The dogs also lie down watching them all, intrigued by their antics. Food lying out not only attracts birds, however, it also attracts rodents.

When working in the house before we moved in, on the landing we found a nut bar we'd left lying out had been nibbled. It appeared that somewhere in the house we had mice. We tried to find where they were living before we were to close up all the walls, but to no avail. The dogs were useless in helping us locate the mice and seemed unaware there were even any creatures living in the house.

We decided to set a humane trap loaded with a piece of the little creature's favourite snack bar and waited quietly downstairs to see whether anything happened. Not that day, but the next, when we repeated the procedure, after about half an hour we heard the humane trap's door close. In great anticipation, we raced to see what we'd caught. And there, looking through the Perspex at us, was a brown wood mouse with his big, nocturnal vision eyes widened; he was clearly in shock at his unexpected incarceration. We located a safe place for him and went off to put him among the moss and stones of an old derelict building in the garden. There were many places for him to find food and to hide from predators. We left him some food to start him off on his new journey, including a piece of his favourite nut bar. And off he scurried into the gaps and dark, green, furry moss between the old, grey stones.

Over the coming days, we caught four more wood mice, and then began to wonder whether it was the same one, laughing at us as he made off with his tasty snack, and then returning the next day to go through the same thing again. A few years before, someone we know had suspected the same and had applied a small dot of paint to the tail of what they thought was their fifth captured mouse. Right enough, the same mouse returned!

Instead of doing that, we searched the outside of the house and discovered a hole which had been made by the heating engineers when they'd installed the air source heat pump. It was tiny, but just big enough for an itsy-bitsy rodent to head into the warmth beside the pipes. Knowing no creatures would be trapped in there as it led into the house, Alun blocked it up. Later that day, we caught one more wood mouse – and then no more. All of this went by without a peep from the dogs that there had been anything amiss. Shortly, we were to discover that the wood mice were not the only rodents loitering in our midst.

Chapter Eight

Instincts

Our garden wildlife repertoire was to be widened. It all began with a rat, and a pretty ordinary rat, at that. A 'sewer rat' they tend to mostly be known as. I suppose that's mainly because of their penchant for inhabiting the dark tunnels beneath our cities, and the way in which they linger around the drains, allegedly waiting to pounce on us.

They are the stuff of horror films. We are wired to loathe them, be frightened of them, to see them as vermin. We are encouraged to look the other way when the rat catcher comes and dispatches the rats – because they are a nuisance, and they cause disease. Indeed, this one was strutting around the garden as though he (or she) owned the place, and there's long been evidence that they carry some zoonotic diseases, most famously leptospirosis – a horrible bacterial infection, which can be fatal.

But can we live happily alongside them? I think so, is the tentative answer, especially if they have their space and we humans and canines have ours, but what follows is what happened on our unanticipated rodent journey. It was a journey which involved all sorts of rat liaisons, not least between them and our canine friends.

People will tell you all sorts of ways of controlling them, many of which are extremely inhumane and result in the unfortunate demise of the rat. The humane methods either don't work reliably well, or still leave you wondering about how the rat might be getting along with your new rat-repellent plant/device/whatever other (humane and not resulting in the death of the rat) contraption has been used.

And so, the rat in question, she (as we later discovered she was, rather than the 'he' we'd assumed when giving the name Roland), like the rabbits, had perhaps been part of a colony living around there for years as the cottage and surrounding garden and buildings had been deteriorating. For decades, the ground had been covered with nettles, ground elder and briars. To this rat, I suppose, we were the imposters trespassing on their land.

The first day we saw him (her), Connor exclaimed, 'I just saw a rat!' Intrigued, the three of us piled around the kitchen window to wait patiently to see whether said rat would reappear. And, within minutes, between the wooden panels of the fence, out popped Roland.

My heart leapt! What was that feeling? Was that the indoctrinated fear that was taught when I was growing up. Was it Mum or school that did that? Was it TV, or the books I chose to read as a teenager? Was it James Herbert's series of books about these long-tailed rodents, for instance? I must have started reading those books when I was thirteen – way too young.

How did I even get hold of horror books then? Was Mum not watching over me properly? If she were still alive today, I would sincerely tell her off for her bad parenting!

But then, Connor has told me many tales of the horror films he watched when he was still of school age, and Alun and I were sleeping. My teenage horror books had become mirrored by his night-time viewing of the likes of Japanese horror such as the Ring series, Ichi the Killer, and Battle Royale. But can Mum and I be forgiven for our alleged parental mistakes when he went on to gain a PhD in film philosophy and I eventually followed my dream of writing books (although I've yet to find my way into the horror genre).

The fear of rodents is irrational – and completely unfair to rats, especially as I'm someone who has had rats as companions and handled hundreds of them when working in rescue, and then in practice as a veterinary nurse. The kind of rat James Herbert wrote about was Rattus rattus, aka the ship rat, or black rat. And despite the late James Herbert's description of the rats in his books as being small dog sized (just imagine), they're smaller than the brown rat – but, like them, they also carry diseases.

There are giant rats, notably the giant pouched rat of sub-Saharan Africa. They are up to eighteen inches in body and head length combined, and they have a tail of about sixteen inches, but they're specific to Africa. I'm sure those giant ones are very nice, being much like small dogs themselves. I wonder whether James Herbert's horror imaginings influenced the way in which we look at rats, just as the book and film of Jaws affected how we should feel about sharks.

What is the difference between the rats in our gardens and outbuildings, and the ones rat fanciers give a home to? Well, very little, actually. All the rats that people have in their homes as beloved companions are descended from Roland's ancestors, Rattus norvegicus – the Norwegian wild rat. The wild brown rats are just as cute, but are quite likely to bite in defence if cornered. Domesticated rats will, too, but it is far more likely in those wild ones.

In one of the larger veterinary practices in which I worked, there were huge bins at the end of the drive, and each evening we would draw straws to see who was going to take the rubbish out, as there were often what appeared to be massive (James Herbertesque) rats lurking above the bins. I had, of course, by this time already read all the James Herbert series of books about rats, so all my imaginings of wild rats were amplified, especially on dark, misty nights. Once at the edge of the bin enclosure, with a torch in one hand, we would toss the bag over the metal gates which enclosed the bins.

And then run!

One time, I opened the kitchen door at work

and one of them was lurking on top of a bin bag someone had left there earlier. Horrified, I slammed the door as hard as I could.

At first, Ralph and Nell didn't seem to notice there was an imposter rat dwelling in the garden. Perhaps that was our first error, in not wondering why they didn't notice. In hindsight, their lack of interest at that point suggests Roland had always been there – had become a part of the garden 'furniture'! Perhaps the dogs hadn't been interested because Roland's scent was everywhere, simply because he'd been there all along. Roland wasn't new to them, so why would they bother to react? They didn't react, even when from the window, we watched as Roland began to have a series of visits from another rat. I tried to see whether this was another female, but they moved too quickly. We naively thought, well, they're group-living, so they're probably just sharing the food source.

We would encounter them from time to time, running across the garden as we opened the back door. There were also closer encounters, such as on the day when gardening, we rolled back a long, large rock in the rockery, and there, staring at us, was a brown rat. The rat scurried away. Because of our sheer size, we humans must be very frightening to them. Luckily, Nell was over on the other side of the garden at the time, preoccupied by next door's pile of logs, which she was sniffing through the fence. Were there rats living there, too? I wondered.

To stop a population explosion, we realized we had to nip the situation in the bud. The first thing for us to do was to prevent them from thinking the bird food was a free-for-all, because it seemed they were here for the seeds and nuts. Information on the web pages of animal rescue and avian charities contained lots of advice about how to deal with rats without killing them. And so, we set to work creating barriers around the food table, and we stopped scattering any food on the ground.

The charities also had advice about how to prevent rats from feeling entirely at home in the garden. Delighted to see there were plants which discouraged them, we planted the suggested rat-repellent herbs and shrubs. We planted catmint, lavender, and rosemary. Snowdrops, elderberry, and daffodils we already had in abundance, and interestingly, there were none of those near where the rats were living. There were others, such as geraniums and marigolds we could have tried, but it would be months before those would be available. And so, we sat back and watched and waited. Were the plants effective? Well, it seemed as though they weren't, not really, as we observed Roland and friend happily interacting around the newly planted shrubs, and even standing on top of them. Perhaps the plants would work better once they were more established, we hoped.

And then, quite suddenly, the dogs began to take an interest in the areas where the two rats were living. Nell, especially, would shove her nose down holes we were discovering, and I suppose in the end, there were always going to be consequences of dogs and rats sharing the same vicinity. It seemed there were more rats, and that Roland and friend had had a litter.

We decided to set up a hidden camera and counted six rats. How quickly would this number escalate? They could have several litters a year, depending on the length of the spring and summer and how late in the year it remained warm. With four babies, the population could grow exponentially in just a year.

I felt sick and wanted to return to live in the town – although we'd known they must have been around, we'd never seen rats there. They're always nearby though, aren't they, those rats? Remembering that those were still Covid times, the news, however, began filtering through that there were rat population explosions in the town! Friends near where we used to live were getting rid of their compost bin because they'd seen rats happily running in and out of it. These rats, it appeared, were living under their neighbour's decking, and using the contents of their compost bin as a food source.

The rat population explosion (which for us wasn't an actual population explosion at that point) was happening everywhere. My Aunt Pat, who lives in the city, said she'd seen them crossing the main roads when she was out for a walk with a friend. Even in the city, this was incredibly unusual.

Rodent experts thought it was Covid restrictions which were forcing rats to come out of hiding. Rats' regular routines of cleaning up after us humans had been disrupted, because people were no longer walking to and from work or school, dropping food as they walked. No one was going out for a meal, meaning there was no food waste at the back of restaurants. I suppose it was also a factor that when people had less to do in lockdown, they had become more aware of what was going on in their gardens; everyone was simply noticing more wild rodents.

And so, the rats defied our efforts to discourage them. We really didn't mind them being around, we would have just preferred it if they had gone and lived a little further away from the house because there was plenty of space. The dogs were by then on high alert, especially Nell, who was spending much more time gazing with heightened interest out of the back door and was spending longer outside when she went out there to the toilet. Rats are vulnerable to more than big greyhounds named Nell, however, and much to Nell's delight, local felines also began visiting. They, too, had developed an interest in the rodents – or perhaps it was the catnip, which cats are particularly fond of in a hallucinogenic way, and which we'd planted on the advice of the animal charity's website.

Rats are no match for scheming cats, and dogs like Nell. I must add here that while Ralph was interested, it was not so much that he was planning on doing anything about the rat population – he was interested in them in more of a canine-rodent observation way. We weren't planning on doing much either and hoped the plants and the rat-proof bird table would discourage them, or at least stop them from more breeding. We were silently worried where the experience was taking us, looking online for more humane solutions before our situation perhaps became a huge problem.

The local felines were quite blatant about their presence being all about self-nominated rodent control, and we witnessed them on the night vision camera calmly catching a few unsuspecting rats. And then Nell caught one and immediately dropped it on the ground one afternoon when we were out working in the garden. The rat fled for his life as Nell looked over at us in dismay. I think she didn't know what to do with it once she'd caught it – that chase instinct in her seemed not to have extended to a killer instinct, we thought. But then another rat was not so lucky, as it met its end between her long, greyhound jaws. We told her to drop it, but it was too late. As far as we know, that was the only one she deliberately killed.

Another day, she found one and was chasing the poor creature across the garden. Alun was mowing the grass at the time, and, unfortunately, the rat ended its days not between the jaws of a canid, but in the jaws of the lawnmower. Alun felt dreadful, Nell didn't seem too bothered. I think, however, that she actually had no comprehension of what had just happened. There had been a rat, she hadn't caught it, it was dead. And me? I'd decided I hated country living and, again, wanted to go back to the town.

Amid all this, the rats were not entirely guilt-free. One morning, just after having fed the birds, I looked out of the window and from the corner of my eye, thought I saw a rat grab a chaffinch and scurry off with it. I was astounded, and thought I must have imagined it. The next day, once the bird food was out, I stood and watched. Within ten minutes, a rat managed to overcome all our rat obstacles, got on the rat-proof (or so we thought) table, grabbed a little yellowhammer, and jumped off the table with the poor bird secured in its mouth.

I was traumatized, and wondered when all this death and destruction would end! And so, we set to work building an even more rat-proof table, with a rubber 'skirt' around it so they couldn't hop from the legs of the table onto the top where the birds were feeding. A few days later, one Houdini rat managed to overcome our efforts by swinging on the rubber skirt and flipping himself over and landing on the tabletop. Luckily, it seemed he wasn't the bird-killing rat and was only up there for the nuts, grains, and delicious seeds.

We'd observed as many as ten rats, and through a series of events (cats, Nell, and lawnmower, and I'm sure the odd rook or bird of prey had had their fill), we had found ourselves down to just three – a mature male and two youngsters.

The day after that last dog-rat event, however, we discovered something about the structure of the rat society that existed in our back garden. It seemed that Nell's lawnmower plus rat incident had taken out what can only be described as a keystone rat – one which was probably the rat who had been taking care of the babies. Many babies, as it happened!

As I glanced up from putting together all the ingredients for my intricately and obsessively prepared morning fruit and nut laden porridge, my heart, I am sure, skipped a beat. Outside, running along the top of the fence, the bar across the bottom of the fence, all over the rocks and plants in the rockery, and underneath the bird table, were no fewer than thirteen baby rats.

I was distraught, and very quickly I realized what must have happened. Over the previous two days, with the lawnmower incident and the other Nell incident, it seemed she had inadvertently finished off the two mums. We hadn't even known there were two mums, as they had kept the babies well hidden. With them gone, hunger must have driven these half-grown rats to desperate measures, as out of their nests they poured in a desperate bid to find food for themselves. The large male lived at the bottom of the garden, well out of our general day to day sight, but later that day we saw him out feeding with them – his paternal instincts and drive to ensure the survival of his species overcoming his normally wise absence. Any sign of anything scary and they all scarpered – him to his safe lair away from us, and all the babies under the fence to the trees in the BG.

We considered feeding them (after all, our dog had killed at least one of their parents), but chastised ourselves for even thinking such a thing, especially as it appeared they were perfectly capable of finding food for themselves. And, of course, we didn't want to exacerbate an already exacerbated problem. But what to do? We'd been thinking that the rat population had been in the hands of the predator-prey race. And yet, there was what could only be described as a paternally led rat creche going on under our noses.

They were cute – very cute. We were surrounded by cuteness overload even. And yet, we couldn't have a situation whereby none of our friends or relatives would dare to venture beyond the garden gate. Already some friends on garden visits had seen one or two of them scurrying across from A to B, and, of course, in my mind was that innate worry about disease.

We were only in July – if it stayed warm, the females would grow and probably have their first litters that year.

They were clever, too, those baby rats, because they instinctively knew the difference between Nell and Ralph! If it was a nice, sunny day, and Ralph was lying outside on a dog bed we'd strategically placed for him so he could soak up the sun (with sun cream on his white muzzle and bald chest), the rats would come out and do their food-searching acrobatics while he lay there. As soon as Nell appeared, they would scurry away and not come out again until she had gone. They were clearly watching and waiting from their tunnels near the rockery. They seemed to know instinctively that Ralph was a gentle giant who would be interested in them in a curiosity kind of way and not a predatory one.

But, still, all those rats were capable of breeding. In desperation with our love-hate relationship of our resident rodents, we looked up one of our last resort devices – the ultrasonic rat repellent. On researching them, it became apparent that they can cause all sorts of side-effects such as nausea, and where would the rats go? Would it harm them? And what about the birds – in a completely speciesist way, we wanted them to stay? What about the dogs? What about the horse who lives just twenty yards away from one side of our garden? Neither dogs nor horse had an option of packing their bags and relocating. No, it was unfortunately not an option.

While we were still thinking about what to do, if anything, given the way in which on our night wildlife camera we were witnessing the local cats annihilating all manner of wildlife in the garden (I love cats, but some are like killing machines), the situation was slowly resolving itself, and we were back down to just a few rats. They would need to battle on through the winter, which would reduce their population. We decided they'd had enough – they already had enough to deal with, and relocation or whatever solution we thought about, would only add to their problems. But then, as we settled into the cooling weather, there was still more to come in the unfortunate saga of the rats.

One early autumn, miserable, rainy afternoon, from the kitchen window I could see Nell in the garden. I figured Alun must have let the dogs out to go to the toilet between the showers. I concentrated hard on what she was doing. She was pawing at the ground. In front of her, I could see what looked like a lump of mud. And then, it dawned on me, I realized it was a dead rat. Had she just killed a rat? Feeling sick, I rushed outside and called her away, but she was insistent, pawing at the motionless lump on the ground. But this was no Nell-dispatched rat. The little corpse was stiff, its tail straight, its legs curled. At the tiny, pointed, whisker-framed nose, I could see blood around the nostrils, there was more blood around the anogenital region.

Warfarin.

I'd seen it many times while working in veterinary practices – mostly in dogs who'd come across the poison, but also some wild animals, mostly foxes. I swiftly removed the rat from Nell, lest she picked it up and tried to eat it. Warfarin kills animals by making them bleed to death, and over the coming days we were to find several rats, a wood mouse and two rabbits which had been poisoned – that tell-tale, crusted blood evident around their mouth and nose.

With animals brought to the clinics because of accidental poisoning, the vets were able to administer the antidote, vitamin K, but there was no one around to save these creatures as their small bodies gave up.

In addition to this, the rabbits were having a tough time with another rabbit problem, as we began finding rabbits with myxomatosis. The virus was deliberately unleashed on rabbits in the 1950s to control their population. And so, over the coming weeks we found several myxomatosis rabbits dead or dying. For weeks, it felt as though we were living in an animal graveyard. My thoughts of returning to town-living returned.

It was the beginning of November and we'd been living in the cottage for almost a year. From the window, I caught sight of a rat shifting from beside the gnarled hawthorn trunk to a hole he must have made between the rocks in the rockery. Against all the odds, it seemed that one of them had survived. The rat looked like a young adult and was probably one from the mid-summer litter; the new year would no doubt bring a new generation of rats to conquer our garden and battle against predators, devices, and the toxins humans have created to defeat them. With all their hardships, some rabbits had also survived to struggle on through the winter.

The year for us, however, was going to close with a new member of the family, one of the canine variety. As if the creatures in the garden hadn't already got enough to contend with.

Chapter Nine

A New Canine Playmate

I'd watched Swift from the day he appeared on the rescue shelter web page. I had been looking for a few months, occasionally wafting my phone with an image of a sad-looking, homeless dog in front of husband, son, brother, or anyone else who would look. His description seemed perfect – he was male, which, given Nell's behaviour around fellow female dogs, would surely be a positive thing?

I weighed having another male dog in our lives against our previous thoughts that Ralph might not appreciate having another male around. We reminded ourselves that when living in the town, all Ralph's best buddies had been male: Buster, Chester, Alfie, and Dexter – how could we have forgotten that? Perhaps when deciding Nell was the most suitable dog at the time, we had been short-sighted in thinking he wouldn't have liked to have had some male canine company around.

The heading of Swift's adoption page stated he was a Gentle Soul, and as I looked into his big, brown eyes, he absolutely had an air of gentleness about him. He looked quite saluki-like, but there was clearly some cross in him too. His ear fur was fluffy, and his muzzle not so long, but somewhere in his mixed ancestry there was, I was sure, probably saluki. But it was, indeed, that heading which told me he was gentle – that trait was what I was sure would fit with Ralph and Nell.

His description said he was very timid, easily spooked, and that he needed someone to help build his confidence. Surely having been through all our experiences with Ralph, we could be those people. They said he liked other dogs and walked nicely on the lead, but that they wouldn't recommend he be let off lead until he had bonded with someone.

With him having been brought to the kennels as a stray, there was no history for Swift, and anything they knew about him had been what they'd discovered through his behaviour and interactions with the staff and other dogs. He was a bit of a psychological mess – there were going to be no cuddles and licks for us if we were to bring him home. He was going to need patience, time, and plenty of understanding.

In so many ways I knew we were the home he needed, but for several reasons, it was the wrong time. We were still working on the cottage, as while much of the house itself was finished, we still had builders putting up our extension, which once built, would mean more indoor space for all of us. And so, I kept on longingly watching Swift on the charity's web page, wondering what he was like, where he'd been before, and how he'd found himself in that predicament. I optimistically thought that at least the extension would be finished soon, so perhaps we could bring him home, but then delays meant it wasn't. He was a quite unusual-looking, yet handsome dog – surely someone would snap him up soon, I hoped.

Still, I kept on watching him, and nothing happened. Weeks passed, and I realized my little fantasy of Swift coming to live with us had not been shared with Alun. Connor knew, and I'd even sent a screenshot picture of him to my brother via WhatsApp, but I knew Alun would be the one to convince. I continued to look at Swift's picture every day to see whether anyone had reserved him. But no, he was still there, all leggy and pointy-faced, and gazing out of the computer at me, and me into the computer at him. Images of dogs around him were labelled 'reserved,' while his photograph remained with no such label, and thus no sign of adoption on the horizon.

One Thursday evening after dinner, I could no longer hold my thoughts to myself – yes, we had the builders in, but Ralph didn't like the builders either, so we consistently shielded him from the noise. It would be just as easy to shield two nervous dogs from the rumbling and banging. Nell wasn't bothered about the builders, seeing them as more of an inconvenience to her routine than something to be wary of. Ah, yes, Nell, the other main reason for my hesitancy. She was a bit particular about other dogs, but as time had gone by, I told myself, she'd mellowed.

My request for a new dog to join us was met with a surprising degree of acceptance. Had I dropped so many hints that it had been expected? Were those three dog emoticons strategically placed on the end of all my messages working some kind of subconscious magic? Was it the pre-retirement wish I'd shared in which we'd have three dogs again coming to the fore? Or was it my perfect timing on a day in which Alun had had a particularly good day up in the hills with the wind turbines? The decision was agreed by all of us that we were ready to go back to having three dogs, and I could hardly sleep that night.

Later that evening, I noticed Swift's photograph had appeared on Instagram above a hashtag saying he was #lookingforlove! What if other potential families were planning to phone as soon as the shelter switched their phones on at 10.30 am the next day? I lay in bed, excited that having him come and live with us was a possibility. Coupled with that excitement, though, was the worry of the undeniable fact that bringing any new dog into your home creates upheaval.

Every dog we'd ever brought home (bar one, I think, and that had been good old solid and level-headed Dillon, Connor's old growing-up dog) had arrived with some issues. Some of them had arrived with many problems… all of which had to be unraveled piece by piece, and heartrending, complicated issue by issue. When you bring home a rescue dog you don't always expect an easy ride. But I think that this also applies to a puppy because how that puppy is treated in those first few months contributes greatly to shaping their outlook for the rest of their life.

The following morning, at precisely 10.30 am, I phoned the kennels. My heart was pounding as I began to ask about Swift. He was still available! No one had shown any interest in him. The kennel assistant sounded as excited as I was because she'd been the main person taking care of him. Just as they'd described in the blurb on his adoption page, he was apparently extremely nervous; he was frightened of people but loved other dogs. That was a good start with Nell, I thought to myself, as I was sure she wouldn't tolerate any aggressive tendencies. I arranged for us to go and meet him.

Because of the by then third wave of Covid restrictions, so that no one turned up unannounced, the shelter was operating a strict appointments system. We were to wait two days to go in to meet him: two days, which would mean two more sleepless nights! For him, it would mean two additional nights in the shelter. In my mind, despite the fact we'd not yet met him and, more importantly, Ralph and Nell had no idea what was going on, he was already one of the crew – part of our family. I only hoped that little sense of doubt about rushing into things, as is my wont, would not this time backfire on me.

Two more nights with little sleep, and I lay there both nights thinking about him and the world in which he'd found himself. He was safe in the shelter, but we wanted to give him safety and happiness – somewhere to play and somewhere to rest his troubled head; somewhere he could call his own.

Sunday afternoon couldn't come quickly enough. Alun was on call and was called into work to get a wind turbine working, so unfortunately couldn't go with us – and given Swift's nervous nature, for that first meeting, we decided to leave Ralph and Nell at home.

On the Sunday afternoon, accompanied by one of the people from the shelter, he emerged warily across the quadrangle courtyard of the kennels. Dogs barked from behind the walls – deliberately hidden from the public to reduce their stress levels and to prevent visitors from wanting to take dogs home on a whim.

Swift was surprisingly smaller than his leggy images on the website had suggested. I wondered what genetic miracles had resulted in him being so saluki, and yet about eight inches shorter. His brindle was in the deepest, richest ginger and black bands, and underneath his tail he had long strands of saluki-feathered fur. Long, fluffy hairs shrouded his ears, and fluff cushioned the spaces between each of his toes. Could he actually have been a collie crossed with a whippet, and have no saluki heritage at all? I wondered.

Connor and I sat on the frosted winter tarmac to allow Swift to greet us when he was ready. I lowered my head and averted my gaze from him, just as I had done with Ralph in that very courtyard more than ten years earlier.

Waiting.

Surprisingly, he came straight over and sniffed at my hair. We both held out dog treats to entice him to stay. He took them from us, oh-so-gently, delicately taking each one between his upper and lower incisors. He was very sweet. His fur was soft but very dry, nothing that a low-stress environment and healthy food wouldn't improve.

We were allowed to take him for a wander through the small woodland the kennel staff and volunteers had planted some years earlier. We strolled along autumnal leaf-coated paths which were flanked by nearly naked trees, the winter sun was low in the bright, blue sky. A wintry breeze nipped at our noses and fingers, as we tried to get to know our shy new friend. We walked around the tree-lined route several times, pausing now and then to give him treats, or just to talk to him.

Swift's focus was not on us, but on the other dogs walking by. Each dog was lost, having been abandoned or relinquished from the world they had known before; after all, they had all known some other life. But circumstances beyond the control of these canines resulted in them being set aside. They were all lucky to have ended up in a shelter that would do their utmost to find them a new family. Not all unwanted dogs find themselves in such a halfway house. In both Swift and Ralph's cases, they were put out on the streets to fend for themselves – the people who were meant to look after them leaving them in a dangerous world where anything could have happened to them. They could have been hurt or killed in a road traffic accident, in which people might also have been hurt or killed. The irresponsibility, lack of compassion, and sheer stupidity of some people makes me despair.

The name the shelter had given Swift was not a reference to our avian friends, but more the sheer speed at which he could run – and run away if he had the opportunity. He had already escaped from the kennels once when being loaded into a car on his way to the vet clinic. They found him not so far away, having invited himself to a barbecue in the garden of a local family. Not surprisingly, they wanted him to have a home with a secure garden, and they also said he would probably not be too keen on cats. With Nell (and Peggy before her), we'd certainly become used to dogs who weren't keen on cats.

Swift loved other dogs, after all, that was one of

the reasons why we thought he would be happy living with us. As we ambled along with him, when he saw those other dogs from the kennels walking by, he did somersaults (practically turned inside out to do so) in excitement. The kennel staff had warned us he would. He was strong, and while we'd imagined a fluffy version of Ralph with a Ralph-like temperament, this was no Ralph – just as Nell was nothing like Peggy had been.

Swift was clearly wary of people, but there were no calming signals that day – not a yawn, no lip licking, no turning away, no stretches to bide his time while he decided whether we were a threat, or to let us know he was no threat to us. He violently cowered away, however, if we tried to touch him, recoiling, making himself as small as he could.

This was a dog who had been hurt, and hurt badly, be it by the people who were meant to take care of him and who let him stray (perhaps deliberately abandoning him in a strange town), or by the people he came across on the streets. We could only imagine his story and be thankful that along the way someone managed to catch him and was able to take him somewhere that he would be safe.

Swift's days as a stray were more than a hundred miles away, his place of safety was with our local rescue kennels. And we hoped that we, along with Ralph and Nell, were going to be the ones to take over from the staff at the shelter, in letting him see that life could be okay; we were desperate to show him that there could be a happy ending.

But first, he was to meet the aforementioned Ralph and Nell. Ralph, we suspected, would be a little grumpy at first, but he would be okay – it was Nell who really needed to accept him. We arranged to take the two of them to meet him. Because the shelter was busy with appointments, the soonest we would be able to go back was two days later.

When those two days had passed, with some trepidation, we headed off to the kennels with Ralph and Nell loaded into the back of the car. This was a long-term commitment, Swift would be around us for the rest of his life – he was young and if he remained healthy, he would outlive both other dogs. His time with us would traverse them and possibly future dogs, and he would need to get along with all of them.

On first sight of him, Ralph and Nell were curious but there were no signs of aggression. With the shelter assistant walking Swift, we took them for a walk around the kennel woods, and then into a field where we could have let them all off lead for a run about, but it was too soon, especially for Nell. All three dogs first needed to take time to get to know one another on lead. This was something we could do away from the super-charged kennels environment. But this was Swift's chance for a bit of exercise, and he was allowed to run around off lead on a loose long line while the other two watched.

He was super-excited and running around like there was no tomorrow, burning off his pent-up energy. Meanwhile, Nell was conflicted – did she like him? Did she want to bite him? She was certainly lunging at him as though if he came any closer, she would do exactly that. But she was also wagging her tail. We couldn't let her off, not then, as her chase instinct was too strong, it really was too soon. Meanwhile, Ralph was petrified.

When Swift's battery was finally out of charge, there was some calmness while he caught his breath. I suggested to the shelter assistant we stop for the day because everything at that point had become calm – we needed to finish on a positive note. While Nell's lunging had been expected given the circumstances, it was also disappointing. Would Swift really fit in with her and Ralph? As the shelter assistant pointed out, because she lived with Ralph, Nell was clearly happy to live with another dog, it would probably just take a bit of time to introduce them properly. We just hoped this meant she would be happy living with two other dogs. In my mind I could already visualize young Swift lying on the sofa and opening his present at Christmas. He was younger than some of the dogs we had considered (I had considered!), but it was the description of his temperament which suggested he might fit in. And I hoped with so much of my heart that would be the case.

Two days later, we were back at the kennels to take the three of them for another walk together. Alun was able to join us that time, and so we headed off for a long walk down the lane towards the river. It was a beautiful, crisp, sunny winter's day. There were many opportunities for the three dogs to sniff together along the way; simultaneously taking in the scents from the same clumps of grass or plants where many a dog had urinated, was good for bonding.

Just twice, Nell gave him a sidelong look to warn him to keep away from her face, and on one occasion she snapped at him. At that point we were nearly back at the kennels, and we could all hear the dogs barking, all feel the heightened tension – perhaps it was just that? We hoped so. We decided we needed to get the three of them away from the kennels environment as soon as possible so we could take the introductions at our own pace. Swift was nervous of us all, and the other two were nervous about being at the kennels. Ralph had come from there ten years earlier, and we were sure he remembered, or at least sensed something fearful.

The shelter manager agreed it would be better for them all if we took him home to continue with careful introductions. There was a severe storm with weather warnings predicted for later that night, so it was better to go back that day, rather than leave him there until the Saturday. And so, we took the other two home so we could prepare for our new arrival. Later, while Alun remained at home to wait with Ralph and Nell, Connor and I returned to the kennels with Swift's collar, identity disc, harness, and lead.

Swift's disc bore his new name: Mads, which is a Scandinavian name, shared by Mads Mikkelsen, the great Danish actor. We felt Mads had a little resemblance to his Danish counterpart. He hadn't responded to the name Swift, so we had felt it was okay to change his name to something which didn't even have the same sound. The name Mads is pronounced 'Mass' with a silent 'd' but he would be called Mads with the 'd' pronounced. Its UK equivalent is Matthew or Matthias.

With the paperwork signed, we bundled Mads and his skinny, long-undernourished body into the car, and arrived home just as the blue sky was starting to gather the blackest of fast-moving clouds.

The storm was on its way – in more ways than one!

Chapter Ten

So, He's Staying Then?

Our first evening walk with the three of them had us returning to the safety of the house after only fifty yards. It was 9 pm and the predicted storm – Storm Arwen – was already wild! Huge, centuries-old trees which would have seen many a storm, were bending in the wind. The ash trees in our garden had already cast aside some of their unwanted branches; more for our rabbit-protecting dead hedge, we thought. It was some humdinger of a wintry, wet, windy storm. As we watched through the window overlooking the back garden, we wondered whether there would be many branches left on any of the trees by morning.

Mads was to sleep in Connor's downstairs part of the house – essentially, he was mainly to be Connor's dog, and we considered that sleeping arrangements should be something established right from the start. He could choose where he slept – two-seater sofa, Connor's bed with him, or the comfortable dog bed on the floor next to the bookshelves. Not surprisingly, as most dogs would if given a choice, he chose the sofa! In Mads' case, it was far too soon for this nervous dog to buddy up with any human – he really was a tortured soul.

And so, Ralph and Nell headed off to bed with us, and Mads to his new shared bedroom with Connor. Mads didn't settle easily – but that was expected. We were strangers, the house was strange, we didn't even know whether he had ever been inside a house.

As expected, and after a restless night for all of us, the new day emerged with much fallout from the night before. The storm had brought down large branches from our trees. As we chatted while we walked around checking for any damage, we acknowledged that we'd introduced a dog with a hugely damaged soul into our lives – Mads was an emotional mess!

The old six-foot fence between ours and a neighbour's house had fallen with the strength of the storm. It was the only fence we hadn't put up in the months after we bought the cottage. It needed to be replaced, but in the meantime, Alun and our neighbour would fix it. The ash trees which tower over our 1880s cottage had flung branches right across the garden, surprisingly missing our cottage and greenhouse, and next door's house.

I was so relieved that when we bought the house, we'd had the foresight to separate the two parts of the garden (so we had a secure garden within what we had thought was also a secure garden), or else that morning after the storm all three dogs could have escaped onto the busy road. That thought is the stuff of my nightmares.

You could tell Mads liked the other dogs, but they were not yet ready for too much buddying up with him. For most of the Saturday after the day of the storm, Nell and Mads were on leads when in the same vicinity – Ralph was left to be Ralph as he was never going to be a threat to anyone, but I could see that even he wasn't too sure about this new entity in his life. Interestingly, though, Ralph was not grumbling and growling in the way he had when Nell had arrived, so that was one factor in Mads' favour.

Handsome but skinny Mads, with his overly visible ribs and protruding spine and hip bones, was terrified of us and cowered whenever we approached him. He was touch-sensitive, frightened of everything in the house, and didn't appear to be house-trained. On waking early, Connor discovered Mads had left piles of cowpat diarrhoea and puddles of urine all over the floor, which Mads had clearly walked through several times, meaning he was covered in and reeked of dog poo.

Poor Mads, the attempted walk the previous night hadn't given him the opportunity to go to the toilet, and neither he nor the other two had had any desire to go into the garden after the failed walk. No amount of persuasion before bedtime would encourage any of them to go over the threshold of the back door into the throngs of almost 70mph winds, the waving trees, and the noisy, spinning wind turbine. At least we generated plenty of electricity that night for the little garden office.

We cleaned Mads up as best we could, which wasn't easy with a dog who was on high alert and racing around the house spreading dog faeces everywhere as we tried to catch him. The kennels had told us he was fast – they hadn't been joking! Having taken the other two humans to hold him and me to wash him, before breakfast we put on all three dogs' harnesses and leads and headed out into the quiet after the storm. The only sounds were from the cars going past, and a tiny sparrow offering a relieved series of chirrups – he and his thirty or more little feathered friends had survived the night tucked up in the eight-foot privet hedge in the front garden. I suppose there are good reasons why tiny birds choose to dwell in cozy privet hedges, instead of turbulent, branch-flinging ash trees.

We walked the dogs to the river and across a playing field. Mads went to the toilet, and we praised him – simultaneously feeling amazed that he had anything left to excrete! He was surprisingly good around traffic. Considering his nervousness, coupled with us living on a main road, we'd expected that would be something we would have needed to have worked on with him. A few trucks went cruising past and he didn't even glance at them. Perhaps he was so overwhelmed by everything else that he felt the trucks were the least of his problems. It's also likely he'd spent some time on the streets before someone took pity on him and called the dog warden.

Once we were back at the house, Nell seemed surprised that he was coming back inside. We took the three of them into the sitting room, and two of us stayed on dog watch, while the other made human and dog breakfasts. At this point, whenever they were in the same room, we still had Mads and Nell on leads – just carefully getting them used to being around one another. In the end, we knew that it would be routines like when and where food would be, when walks happened, when bedtime was, and when humans came and went, which would dictate the structure of our fluffy dog's new life. He needed to learn the routine, and Nell needed to understand that this new dog with fluffy ears was going to be a part of those routines.

But she wasn't having any of it!

We had, in that twenty-four-hour period, ruined her life! She glared at him, and she snarled, revealing those giant, shiny greyhound teeth of hers. Ralph, meanwhile, sat on the sofa trembling. We had ruined his life too. But for us, giving up on Mads wasn't an option. He was staying, and Nell needed to get used to the idea.

And so, that first weekend, we introduced him to the routine of walks, food, treats, play time, and Nell to the fact that Mads wasn't going anywhere. We reassured Ralph by letting him know with lots of love and affection that there was no need to worry, everything would settle.

It would just take time.

Mads' and Nell's leads were bravely taken off at the end of the first weekend, when we realized it was ridiculous that we couldn't go anywhere in the house without having one or the other of them with us. This was while Ralph continued to carefully negotiate his way between everyone. He began to show an interest in Mads, as a new playmate perhaps, but Mads was displaying the most terrible nervous behaviour. It seemed that someone, somewhere, had hurt him, and hurt him badly. He shied away from us in a violent way if we touched his head or back, and he hated any of us being behind him, as though someone had forced him into a cage. He sat in front of us and howled, or he stood and relentlessly barked at us. Bark, bark, bark, bark, bark – it was almost constant.

Ten days in, and we realized nothing was settling! We had not only ruined Ralph and Nell's lives, but we had also ruined our own... Mads had turned into a living, breathing nightmare. It wasn't his fault, he had simply never known a life like the one he had arrived in with us, and it was down to us to put in the time and effort to let him see that life could be okay. He no longer had to fend for himself on the streets, searching for food and shelter, each day facing an unknown set of circumstances, which could quite easily have led to his premature demise on the roads. And he no longer had to be afraid of people – no one was ever going to hurt him again.

Our walks had become horrendous as he violently jumped around on the end of his lead doing dog-on-a-bungee impressions whenever he saw another dog. He even reacted to anyone who was carrying a bag, which he thought from a distance might be a dog. While doing so, he would screech at the top of his voice as though someone was murdering him. But that was the least of our problems, and something we could confront in time. We still didn't know him and what he was capable of, and he didn't know us, and we had to gently break through this barrier he'd put up between us and him. The barrier was like a solid wall which we needed to dismantle brick by brick; without doing that, we wouldn't be able to show him that his new life really was okay.

At home, when Mads wasn't barking or howling (and he had a piercing howl), he was charging around the house, not listening to us, not responding to anything we said, not even looking our way. In addition to this, he cowered if we went anywhere near him, looking very much as though he expected that one of us might reach out and hit him.

The situation reminded me of a story Mum used to tell me about something that happened when she was growing up. Her dad was always bringing animals home that he found on the streets nearby where he worked, and one time he arrived home with an adult cat. Once released into the house, the cat started squealing and went charging around the walls and the furniture and then climbed the curtains. He then went charging around the house until he found an open window and disappeared through it, never to be seen again. It's likely the cat was feral, and that's exactly how Mads was behaving – like a feral animal who had had little or no human contact.

I've had a lot of contact with feral cats because in all the clinics I worked, there was one or another capture, neuter, release scheme whereby charities would bring the cats in to us, already safely inside humane traps. The trick, then, though, was to get the cats anaesthetized without accidentally releasing them from the traps. For the most part, this worked, and we made the whole process as stress-free as we could.

On one occasion, however, a huge male tabby cat escaped from the trap. He shrieked and went charging around the preoperative room, knocking over bottles of injectables, syringes and bandages as he went. We eventually caught him in a huge blanket and quickly managed to sedate him. He was then neutered, vaccinated, and shortly after, just like all the others we had through the clinic, released back to where he had come from – his familiar territory.

And so, when these dramatic, feral-like

spectacles were happening with Mads, just as anyone would with a baby, we ticked off a mental list of things which might have been wrong with him, and methodically worked through them one by one:

Was he hungry? No, he'd just had a big meal.

Was he thirsty? No, there were dog bowls with fresh water scattered around the house. We'd shown him where they all were and seen him drinking from them, so, no, he wasn't thirsty.

Was he bored? No, we'd just been for a walk, and he'd had time when we'd been trying to play with toys with him indoors and outside.

Was he in pain? He didn't seem to be. His extreme actions suggested this was definitely not something he was experiencing.

Did he need to go to the toilet? No, he'd already been outside six times in the previous hour.

Was he missing someone? We assumed if he was, it would be someone at the kennels, rather than someone from his previous life. But, no, unlike with Nell when she first arrived, it just didn't feel that this was his problem, especially as he'd had his own kennel at the shelter.

Mads really was an absolute mess, and amid his behavioural worries was the distinct lack of house training; but like the walking on a lead problem, that would come, we could deal with house training and lead problems later. First, with all of this, he needed to be responsive to us. We needed him to see us as friends not foes, and we also needed him to be willing to work with us to help us to fix him. But it was tiring – none of us were sleeping because the daytime, devil-like (as we had begun to view them) shenanigans continued through the night, and although Connor got the worst of it downstairs, we could also hear him upstairs and would often head down to help.

We continued to be careful with Nell, as we were still not sure what she was thinking – she was playing her greyhound cards close to her chest. We had adopted a dog who was unresponsive to us and unresponsive to Nell and Ralph, and that decision had upset our lives. But we had made that decision and we needed to persevere. It was as though Mads was living in an isolated bubble, and never had any dog we'd lived with been in more need of help – even Ralph.

Mads' running rampage around the house, as well as being similar to how feral cats would behave, I could also liken to the behaviour observed in some footage which I would use in my teaching about the domestication of wolf cubs. A litter was being kept as part of an experiment on nurturing and socialization, to see how their behaviour compared to a litter of puppies the team had previously reared. These wolf cubs ran riot – they had no direction and were clearly not responding to the love and attention being bestowed on them, despite them being cared for during their critical early socialization weeks. Mads was responding how a wild dog would, one who was having domestication forced upon him.

One memorable day in those early few days, while Ralph and Nell lay in judgement on the sofa, heads together, watching and waiting for the next round of antics, suddenly all around us there was chaos. Connor and I were on dog control duty, as it was still taking two of the three of us to keep some level of 'normality' in the house at any given time. Mads was running wild, barking, howling, jumping around, and we'd checked everything on our list of things which might have been up with him, and we were exhausted. And then, eventually, he went and lay down – he'd tired himself out and was physically and mentally burnt out. As he flopped onto the beanbag, Connor and I sighed in exhaustion.

Then, simultaneously, Ralph and Nell sighed too! Their relief at finally having a little peace and quiet was palpable, as they rested their heads down on their paws. We all sat in silence for an hour or so and enjoyed the quiet. Meanwhile, Mads recharged his batteries for the next round of shenanigans.

Chapter Eleven

A Breakthrough

Our breakthrough with Mads, strangely, came in the form of our big, muscular greyhound Nell. We had got to the stage where one of us could take care of the three dogs, and that particular morning it was my turn. Within half an hour, and despite having been walked, fed, and so on, Mads began his morning devilries. After about ten minutes, he went over to Nell and began barking at her – right in her face. Now, Nell doesn't like such encounters with other dogs, and she glared at him. He ran off, and then came back and did it again. I called him away, but he wasn't listening. Despite all the treats and toys we had available for distractions and to encourage interactions with us, he was still not communicating with any of us humans.

And then, Nell, seemingly having had enough, leapt on top of him! I called her off, but she had him pinned to the ground. Alun was at work thirty miles away, Connor was working in his studio at the end of the BG, and I was alone while our big greyhound was attacking (and in her frustration, I thought, perhaps trying to murder) this weedy, scrawny, much smaller than her, infuriating fluff ball.

In panic, I shouted at her and went to grab her collar to pull her off him. But then I held back because I noticed that while, yes, she had him pinned to the ground, yes, she was a good fifteen kilograms heavier than he was, he lay on his back submitting to her, and although she was making gruff sounds, her tail was wagging, as was his. The tail wagging wasn't in that aggressive or apprehensive way, but proper, real happiness. That moment of recognition, of realizing that the dogs knew better than I did, was humbling.

It was a huge turning point, and from that moment, I understood and truly felt that they were going to be all right. They had made a connection with each other and now we humans had to connect with him too.

Once I'd waited for them to finish what was clearly play, I watched as the two of them went over to the water bowl and shared a drink. I knew that from that point things could only get better. It wasn't going to be easy, but we'd had a breakthrough. When they'd had their water, Nell came over to me panting. She looked up at me. If she'd been human, I truly believe she would've said, 'There you go, that's how you do it!' And from that monumental point in our experiences with our new dog, all our lives began to very slowly improve.

The very next day, I received the phone call from the shelter to check on how Mads was doing. I was so glad the call hadn't come even twenty-four hours earlier, because our lives would have still been in disarray. I was able to tell her, honestly, that while we'd been having problems, we'd just turned a corner. There was finally potential for him to be the dog he was always meant to be.

In the coming weeks, we had breakthroughs in abundance. Slowly, but surely, Mads became embedded in our household's routines, albeit he was still not connecting with us properly. He still wouldn't make eye contact, although he did this willingly with Ralph and Nell. He began to understand that he no longer had to search for food, as food would be coming anyway, along with a regimented-style delivery of treats routine. That was a routine which was never going to be relinquished by any astute greyhound named Nell, or lurcher named Ralph. So, guided partly by the routine, but perhaps more by the expectations of Nell and Ralph, and him closely watching their reactions at certain times of the day, things were improving, in the house anyway.

Mental stimulation is vital in a dog – dogs are group-living animals, and in the absence of other dogs in their world, we must fill that space for them. We must be their playmate, their companion, their resting and sleeping buddy, their friend. In doing so, we prevent them from becoming bored or anxious. Middle-aged greyhounds and elderly lurchers laze about a lot – Nell and Ralph drape themselves over any available piece of furniture. Mads demonstrated he was perfectly capable of that draping thing too, but as a two-year-old, of course his need for rest seemed to be much less. In giving him a home, we had made an agreement that we would make sure he was happy. But with a dog who was consistently not really communicating with us, it was difficult to know what to do to help him to feel fulfilled.

Play, though, and finding the type of play he liked, was important, but despite our best efforts, his recall was atrocious, which made off lead play such as fetch and ball games difficult. Enter the long line, the training tool which was to alter his world and ours. The long line is just that, a long lead – usually about twenty feet long. You can use it for all sorts of training such as sit, stay, or wait from a distance and, of course, recall. Apart from helping us with recall, we wanted it to give him an element of freedom in a way which would enable us to catch him more easily when needed i.e., by going for the end of the line, rather than him.

We'd never had a dog for whom we couldn't just open the back door to allow them to go and explore the wonders of nature in the garden, knowing that when we called them, they would come running to us. With Mads, each time we went out with him and allowed him to wander lead-free and explore around the trees and plants (in the regular-sized garden, not at that stage the BG), he consistently refused to come back into the house, seeming incredibly fearful.

So we could get him back inside, each time we

had to invest in an array of things to attract him through the back door – squeaky toys, food, balls thrown from the garden into the house. None would work. And so, all we could do was wait for him to tire himself out, and then gently catch him and put the lead on while he was distractedly sniffing at the plants. He was probably sniffing for rabbits or rodents, but I like to think that he was appreciating our horticultural efforts. Once we had a hold of him, we would give him lots of fuss, all the time showing him that he wasn't going to be punished for anything. We had to do everything in tiny, miniscule steps.

It was heartwarming to see him galloping around the BG on the long line for the first time. From a distance, we could observe his puppy-like wonder with the world, as every now and then he paused to sniff or watch. I couldn't wait for the spring and summer to come, because so much more would be going on in the garden for him to interact with – and it would be warmer, too.

One mild, winter's day, he stopped and looked upwards, as overhead a group of about thirty geese emitted their deep honking sounds while flying over the garden. The lead bird dropped back to take a rest, while another took over. We all watched in silence with him as the birds traversed the winter sky, accurately adjusting their perfect 'V' so they could fly in the wake of each other's swirling wind.

Mads had demonstrated his interest in ornithology early on, when each day in the garden for his morning toileting, he'd frequently been distracted by the rooks and jackdaws as they squawked from the trees; impatiently waiting for one of us to head out with the morning's corvid and little garden bird food supply. The pigeons and doves would always make an appearance too.

Mads immediately loved the pigeons; Peggy was like that too, only with her there was a sort of slyness about how she approached her interest in them. She would creep into the garden, pretending she wasn't interested in the ones who were happily gobbling up the grains we'd put out for them. Sometimes she'd wait ten minutes or more, and then she would ambush them. Not so with Mads – as with everything Mads was doing, it wasn't very dainty or eloquent as he raced towards the poor birds, and they noisily fluttered to the skies to escape his eager mouth and paws.

But amid that complex predator-prey race going on in the garden, the champion potential-prey award had to go to a tiny rodent-like insectivore. When we bought the cottage, the ground looked as though it had been damp for decades and had some areas where bog-loving plants had thrived. We made a conscious effort when we moved here to ensure that we left some areas as we found them, so those plants would survive. With effective drainage some of the areas admittedly became much drier by default, however as they did, little creatures appeared to have moved in, using the plants as cover.

In one of those areas where the reeds were still thriving, one day I spotted Mads focused on and shoving his nose into the reeds. I raced over to see what he was up to (there was no way his then still sporadic recall was going to distract him if there was a creature there). When I got close to him, I saw him raise up on his hindlegs, bring his front paws together and then slam them down onto the ground – just like a fox would. He was definitely in hunting mode, and I quickened my pace to get to him and save whatever unsuspecting creature was trying to hide there.

While I stood beside him trying to see what it was that he was interested in, Mads remained focused on that one spot. I held onto him and separated the reeds to see what might be there and was sure there was nothing. Mads, meanwhile, continued to stare at that one place. I continued to hold him, lest he suddenly pounced again. And then, from the corner of my eye, I spotted a tiny, pointy-faced shrew scurrying along from some other reeds we were standing beside, over to the safety of the next reeds a few feet along from us. And Mads was so focused on the reeds directly in front of him, that he didn't notice a thing! I felt triumphant for the little creature who had made his way to safety; his teeny size and speedy movements had allowed him to escape his potential predator – a predator who had let his collie-like, focused obsession with that one space get in the way of his other instincts.

We don't know what the dogs' living arrangements were before they came to us. Nell, as with most ex-racers, was most likely in a kennel for much of the time. Ralph, too, I'm sure would have been in a kennel, as he seemed to have no concept of home comforts when he arrived with us, and it was likely from all the old wounds on his legs that he was used for hare coursing. With Mads, I'm not so sure, only that if he was in a home, then it was likely to have been a confined space, and he wasn't happy with being around people.

There are steps in rescue dogs' progress which can immediately warm your heart, and one of those things with Mads was the first time he felt confident enough to go and lie on Connor's bed. He had his own sofa, so he could have simply carried on using that, but no, within three months, his confidence had grown to the point that he felt he would sometimes make a choice.

Apart from when we were all sleeping, all the doors connecting the rooms were open, and Mads gradually got used to joining any of us wherever we were in the house, especially Connor or me. With Alun it took longer – mainly because Alun doesn't work from home and is therefore not around so much. You often wonder whether someone in a dog's new life resembles someone in their old life, and then how do you possibly let them know that they're okay now, they're safe, and that no one is going to hurt them?

And then, as spring properly arrived with all its warmth and signs of new life, we had a massive breakthrough! Mads finally began to look at us. His big, beautiful brown eyes were finally seeing, he was no longer cowering, he was happier to have his fur brushed and stroked – and we knew that that was the start of his journey to the more confident dog we hoped he would become!

He was still doing somersaults when he saw other dogs when he was out on the lead, simultaneously screaming as though he was being murdered, but we began to feel it was lessening. With distractions, U-turns, and avoidance of the situation, when it happened the reaction was much less sustained. It appeared to be very much related to 'happy to see a strange dog' excitement and not nervousness. It also didn't seem to be aggression – aggression was never a word you would associate with Mads. He really was, as the shelter's online description about him had stated, a gentle soul.

Chapter Twelve

Choice: Dogs – Our Best Friend, Living Their 'Best Life'

With Mads slowly starting to open up to us, we were grateful for every tiny step. Each rescue dog brings with them a story. A contribution to the story of your own life, as the lives of dog and human harmonize. At no point, however, did Ralph, Peggy, Lucy, Nell, Mads, or any of the other dogs who have filled my life, ever have a choice about who they went to live with. We chose them, as millions of other people choose an animal to share their life in some way or another. Animals have no option – for all those dogs, when we signed a contract with each rescue organization, it was a contract between us and the people at the rescue, each dog has never willingly been a part of the contract.

Where each dog ends up is a lottery. They perhaps spend eight weeks with their mother and littermates before leaving everything they know to be with a family – who may or may not keep them for their whole life. And with greyhounds like Nell, and Peggy of course, their lottery is in whether they win or lose. And even if they are winners, the welfare of racing greyhounds is known to be incredibly poor. Once their winning (and/or breeding) days are over, if not relinquished to rescue, their fate can be devastating – either shipped to another country where welfare laws (if they exist) are even worse than in the UK, or they are euthanized – sometimes not by a vet.

Domesticated animals designated as companions don't have a choice about the progression of their life. Under the command of humans, they're bred and find their way into the pool of animals of the same species, to be chosen by, and then under the influence of the decisions made by such people. We are in control of their birth, their destination, their companions, their living conditions, their provision of water and food and, in most cases, when and how they die. All animals we humans interact with, whether intended as companions, breeding animals, food, sporting, zoo, or working animals, are all at the mercy of whoever oversees them.

Where an animal is born into a wild environment, for the most part, and where people and our activities are not encroaching on their territories, those animals are presented with choices. They can choose where to live, where to feed, where to drink, which mate they prefer. Essentially, a truly wild animal's life pans out in the realm of survival: their existence progresses instinctively and with a certain degree of luck: luck with the environment into which they've been born, and luck with the resources available in that environment.

For a dog born in a domestic setting, a degree of luck is also evident, but for very different reasons. Their birth has usually happened because of some intention on behalf of an owner. Just by its very nature, the term 'owner' implies a hierarchical structure – one which often adversely affects the behaviour and experiences of the dog. Many forward-thinking animal behaviourists and charities are preferring these days to replace the word 'owner' with the word 'guardian' and while some may argue the word 'owner' implies legal obligations, surely the word 'guardian' does this, too?

Dogs' luck is embroiled in who they end up spending their life with. I would argue here that the environment is far less important – dogs are social creatures and appear through the past hundred thousand years, or so, to have forged a mutual acceptance in this alliance with humans, but who those humans are (and their attitude towards dogs' needs) is the key to whether a dog will thrive.

A dog who lives with someone in a one-bedroomed flat, and that person spends all their time with them and exercises them several times a day, is perhaps in a far better position than a dog belonging to someone else who lives in a big house, trots their dog around the block once a day, works full time, and who leaves their dog home alone for much of the time. I suppose that essentially what I'm saying is that it is the bond and amount and quality of time spent with the animal that matters, not how well off someone might be financially.

There is no doubt that, for the most part, dogs who share their lives with kind people live a comfortable life with affection and plenty of food. Where these fortunate dogs are also able to spend some or all of their time with other dogs (after all they are a social species) and their human companions, dogs seem to glean great joy from their domestic arrangements.

Dogs' 100,000 years by our sides have not been in vain and they communicate with us like no other species intercommunicates with humans. They are great observers of our reactions and how we behave. While we are watching them, they watch us right back. All our mannerisms and facial expressions, the slightest movement of our eyes or mouth and whether we smile or frown, our hand and arm movements, our posture, are noticed and noted – dogs take it all on board. They listen out for regular sounds we make, and the sounds around them. They anticipate our next move by watching even our most subtle changes in behaviour; some less subtle, in that they know when we pick up the house telephone, they're not going anywhere for a while. It makes me wonder when I close the lid on my laptop and I see the dogs suddenly spring to life, 'How long have they been waiting for me to do that?'

As I write this, dear old Ralph, who these days rarely plays with toys, was trying to get my attention by sitting in front of me and flinging a soft toy around. Engrossed in what I was doing, I wasn't completely aware of what he was up to. That was not until I became fully aware of him, and watched as he got up and walked out of the room to go and find someone else to give him some attention. With the doors being open between the rooms, he had the opportunity to do that. Had the doors been closed he would have probably gone and slumped in a chair, sighed, and gone to sleep (just as Nell is doing just now across the room from me, but that's normal for her). They all have the choice to (hopefully) fulfil their needs.

But how do we know? How do we even know whether the animals with whom we share our lives are completely happy? This has bothered me a great deal about our own dogs, past and present, until each time I think about it, I conclude that we're doing our best and that their lives are far better than the lives they came from. But is that enough? To be better than before? On social media, there are countless pictures of animals with the hashtag #livinghisbestlife – I've used the hashtag myself, but the idea that they are living their best life is taken from our own point of view. What if they aren't actually living the best life possible for them? What if they could be living better lives?

One thing we try to do as a family is to give the dogs a sense of choice about all sorts of things – for instance we don't have only one water bowl, but four, all in various parts of the house. This is just a simple example of how an animal can choose when and where to drink (and like many dogs, their favourite is a dirty puddle).

Not so much with these three dogs as they like most treats, but with some of our now-deceased dogs we would offer a choice of a few treats at treat time and, I'm thinking of our dear old greyhound friend Peggy now, she in particular would carefully consider which one she wanted. She seemed to know it was a choice and that this would be her treat for that particular treat slot. But is that just my own basic understanding of what was going on? Perhaps she actually expected the rest too, and was always disappointed she didn't get them all? The truth is, though, that however much we try, we don't know for sure what they think – we can only guess, and then simply attempt to do our best, as people who are trying to do whatever we can to keep the dogs happy. After all, they have their entire present and future invested in us.

It is true that they learn our ways, they learn our routines and what each day is likely to consist of. I like to think of them having a tick list and that hopefully they look forward to the next walk or run around, and their next meal. But what if that next meal never comes? What if the dog (like it's possible Ralph or Mads did) finished up with a person who lost interest in them, who decided they were more trouble than they were worth? So very many dogs spend their whole lives trying to please, trusting the person who occasionally throws them scraps of food, for that is all they have ever known. I have seen the skinniest, most neglected dogs respond positively to the most awful people who couldn't care less for them. Is it that dogs do this because they really don't harbour animosity or hatred in the same way that a person might? Do they forgive? It's so very sad that some dogs never know the comfort of a sofa, or the gentle touch of a kind hand, and yet, many of them still trust those who hurt and neglect them.

If a dog could choose, who would they go to live with – would they even choose to have humans as part of their social circle? I imagine history suggests that they would. Indeed, it has been genetically proven that our dogs are descendants of the wolf and that we have a shared history, originating through combined food sourcing, or wolves investigating human communities and our two species being curious about one another. Dogs trust us, and, as such, we have a duty to do our best for them. The dog in our living room is, however, a much-altered species from their wolf ancestor.

Domestication has done much to change them. They have changed physically, and yet the Chihuahua shares the same amount of wolf genetic input that the husky does. Dogs' facial features resemble those of human babies: large eyes and soft features. It is perhaps no accident that people love their dogs so much and, in some cases, they can become substitute children; living, breathing companions to fill the nest with, either instead of having children or once the human children have left home.

Behaviourally, just as they observe we humans so closely, they also respond to us in ways that no other species does. They bark – something it is thought they evolved to continue beyond puppyhood because of their association with people. Wolves don't bark, as such, they yip and howl – there's not the repetitive sound-making that occurs in dogs. Essentially, over thousands of generations, dogs have adapted their vocal repertoire to communicate with us.

They also lick our faces and engage in play activities, both aspects of behaviour that rarely continue in wolves. Licking faces, wolves mainly use for submissive reasons or when regrouping, but in our dogs, this is a behaviour which is much more widely used. Play in wolves is likely to be much more about social bonding and hierarchal standing.

What has been retained in our dogs has been that need for company, be it with canine companions and/or us, as their family. As the years have gone by, I've become increasingly concerned about the bonds dogs make with one another and how many times, through our actions, those bonds might be broken. This can happen at so many stages of a dog's life and, although in most cases there is little we can probably do about it, there are times when it is possible to maintain those bonds. The main example is when dogs from multi-dog households enter shelters, staff doing their best (and I know that many shelters do) to rehome them together. It's tricky, though, because most people will only want to introduce a single dog to their household – just as we have done with all the dogs we've ever brought into our home.

I think that in our case, like most people, we've always had situations whereby when a dog passes away there is just one 'vacancy' which is then filled by a new dog. In hindsight, perhaps when we got Nell there had been an opportunity to home two dogs that were already a pair looking for a home, but the timing was awkward when it was difficult enough to find just one rescue dog.

We've arrived at a point in our relationship with dogs whereby they are established companions in our society, and yet there seems to be welfare problems associated with our perception of them, their population, and their role in our families. While across the world millions of dogs are waiting for a home in rescue shelters, many people choose instead to buy a dog from a breeder, and that is a crying shame.

Consecutive governments have attempted to control breeding of dogs, in the knowledge that while there are thousands more dogs being born, thousands will be heading to the executioner's needle as space is made for the next batch of dogs to enter the kill shelters.

Ralph was such a dog on death row, only someone in the rescue shelter he found himself in saw something in him, which meant he was one of the luckier ones. But his fate could easily have been sealed in a much more tragic way if someone hadn't taken a liking to him – if he hadn't been such a handsome and gentle dog, and then had there not been space for him to be moved to our local rescue shelter, where we found him. Greyhounds as well, are bred in astounding numbers, and the fate of Nell, too, could have been awful, should her trainer not have been one who relinquishes their greyhounds to a rescue organization once their dogs have run their last races and are suddenly of no use to their money-making needs.

Some people keep their dog in a dog crate overnight and/or while they are out of the house. Why are they left in this way when confinement denies any animal their behavioural needs? Is the crate a misguided solution some people use to enable them to continue their busy lives with no concern for the dog's mental wellbeing? Is it a way in which people are attempting to control existing or potential behavioural problems?

Beyond this, is there, indeed, a sense of property which induces a sort of cognitive dissonance, and results in a population of dog owners not addressing the welfare issues associated with keeping their dog confined to a cage while they go about their own life? Surely, confinement in a crate exacerbates any existing physical and behavioural problems in dogs. My heart sinks when I see dogs on rescue sites who have somehow ended up needing a home and the blurb states proudly that the dog is 'crate-trained'! What does that even mean? That the dog has been forced to spend hours on end in a cage and has appeared to tolerate it?

If overnight is 8-9 hours, and the dog is then confined to the crate again during the day while the people of the house are at work, and let's be generous and say that one of the people works part time, so is only away for four or five hours a day, then the dog is already spending a lot of their life in a cage. Some may then argue that they are there at weekends. But are they really there at weekends? And even so, is that enough?

Dogs need stimulation, and if we think of Mads and the huge amount of mental stimulation he needs to be content, then the thought of him possibly having had to endure life locked up is awful. And whatever happened to him has had consequences in how he became, and the poor, frightened dog we collected that stormy day from the rescue shelter. When did it become acceptable to confine a dog to a cage? From his behaviour when he arrived, I feel this could be a part of Mads' history, and I dread to think how many long hours he may have been forced to spend – stressed and waiting for someone to come and release him from his incarceration.

Chapter Thirteen

Dogs: Our 'Reciprocal' Friendship: or, How We Have Helped Each Other and How We Can Help Them

It is no great accident that the main two species we humans have 'chosen' to share our lives with are dogs and cats. It's believed that the history associated with each of our species collided due to a shared interest in food. With dogs it was likely because of access to the food itself, and cats the rodent availability associated with our growing of crops.

Among other things these two species have since contributed towards our society, are a vast reduction in feelings of loneliness, a support system for children in dealing with all kinds of emotional worries associated with growing up – even in dealing with loss, because after all, the animals in our lives have a much shorter life expectancy than most people do. They also have a proven effect on us in reducing blood pressure and improving heart health. When we think about how we are with them, and they are with us, they have surely been responsible for the gradual change in attitude towards animals in general, especially when a growing number of people have begun to see all animals as being worthy of choice and freedom and seeing them all as someone, not something.

There is also a closeness that we feel when dogs and cats are in our presence, which softens us and makes us better able to cope with the pressures of modern society. The wolf and the African wild cat have come a long way from their wild beginnings to establishing themselves as such a solid part of our lives and, in some parts of the world anyway, we have created a society in which dogs and cats can live in relative safety, protected by their human guardians.

But what is in this relationship for them? How can we make dogs' lives better? Dogs are very much social animals – it's a behavioural trait that is embedded in their very nature. Most dogs would cope better in a household with at least one other dog, but in the absence of another dog, they need us humans to be around for them. They hate isolation and can become extremely lonely – even if that isolation becomes part of their daily routine.

Some dogs are kept outdoors, and I'm sure Nell could tell a tale or two about that. I have encountered many dogs over the years who have spent much of their time in outdoor kennels, many of them single dogs living a lonely, bored, inactive life. Like crates, for the dog this is a huge problem, in that kenneled dogs are not having their needs taken care of. They may have food, water, shelter, but these are sociable animals, and in the absence of other dogs for company, we should be there as much as possible.

A dog kept outside is at risk from extreme

weather (hot or cold) and is at risk of being stolen. I'm sure none of these dogs would choose to live their life away from people and other dogs. If choice is a welfare issue, then it's the legislation about our relationship with dogs which should change.

Some might argue that a dog in a crate or outdoor kennel is not in a barren environment as they are perhaps left with a food toy and they have a blanket and water, but how long does it take to devour the food from a food toy? Well, if you're Mads, who gets a food toy when he goes and lies on his sofa at bedtime, it takes just three minutes to devour the contents of his toy. Three minutes! That means a dog who is in a crate or left outside for a 'modest' four hours (under UK government guidelines they suggest it is acceptable to leave your dog home alone for no longer than four hours without a break), then the dog has nothing to keep them occupied for the other three hours and fifty-seven minutes while they wait for their people to come home! The other two dogs aren't interested in food toys, not seeming to see the point of them – these greyhounds and greyhound types don't like expending any energy unless it's vital to their existence.

Some dogs develop stereotypical behaviours if they're in regular confinement or are bored. These sometimes manifest as an obsession with a particular part of the body, causing self-injury; other times it is a repetitive behaviour. With

Nell, it was her obsession with chewing the tip of her tail; with Mads, it was an obsessive pulling at his own claws – usually his dew claws – almost as though he would pull them from the nail bed. He'd grab hold of one of his dew claws and obsessively tug it and tug it. We would stop him by distracting him with toys or treats when he was calm and not engaging in such a strange behaviour. On examining them, he had clearly been doing it before he came to us, as they were very sore right from the start. I applied a strong-smelling hand cream to discourage him from doing it, but in the early months he would start doing it again once the cream had rubbed off.

Repetitive behaviours in caged animals are disturbing for us to observe, but more importantly, for the animal they are often the consequence of long-term suffering. They are a significant example of the close link between animal welfare and behaviour, in that they provide visual indicators that suffering is happening, or has occurred in the past. Is it frustration? Is it some strange, conflicted behaviour? Is it self-perpetuating, in that there is perhaps something far more complex taking place? Perhaps it is something with a deep-rooted motivation which enables the animal psychological release from their stressful life – something which is, quite paradoxically, enabling them to cope?

These abnormal behaviours can often continue

even after an animal has been removed from the stressor that it is thought caused the behaviour, e.g., from being in confinement or from living a solitary existence if they are a social species. The fact that stereotypies can continue in this way once they are out of the situation, meant that in both Nell's and Mads' cases, there was the potential for their behaviour to have continued in perpetuity, no matter what we did in terms of making sure their lives were enriched.

The self-injurious behaviour both Nell and Mads were doing, varied in terms of their location on the body and their severity: Nell's was ultimately short in duration but severe in terms of damage, and Mads' was longer in duration but less severe in terms of how much damage he did to himself. We could stop him from doing it simply by distracting him and making sure he was always busy – and as we came to know, Mads loved to be busy!

I have nursed dogs with many different types of self-injury, and so when Nell arrived with her chewed tail, my heart sank. Some dogs I have met over the years finished up having their tail amputated because the self-injurious obsession became so bad, and I feared she would be the same. But with care and attention, many bandages, and giving her plenty of other things to think about, she stopped paying attention to her tail, until eventually her wound healed. Along with that healing, the rest of her tail's sparse fur grew back too. Just the other day, I was checking her old racing passport, and on that there's a detailed diagram of where white patches appear amid her mostly black coat. And there, at the tip of the tail on the diagram, it states that hers should be white. With her obsessive behaviour and tail chewing before she arrived with us, she had lost that tail tip, as it is now completely black, bar about three white hairs.

Some animals may inadvertently develop a lick granuloma, which is a raised, raw, red lesion, from their excessive licking of a particular part. These are often on the front leg because this is an easily accessible area when they are lying down. This is thought to sometimes begin because of a lesion elsewhere (which they can't reach), or simply through boredom. Once that behaviour has developed, it can be hard to overcome.

There was a dog I encountered who was confined to a car all day while their owner was at work, and on his paw was the most awful lick granuloma, which the dog's people eventually sorted out with a vet. The dog had to wear an Elizabethan cone for months afterwards, so just imagine the frustration of having developed that behaviour and then having a wound which they couldn't reach. But all this only supports the fact that confinement is never a good thing, and prevention of the development of the behaviour in the first place is a necessary part of our living with dogs.

Thankfully, with both Nell and Mads' stereotypical behaviours, we were able to intercept them by diverting their attention elsewhere, but in severe circumstances when the behaviour has been compounded by long-term incarceration, the animal might need medication and a lot of carefully planned environmental and life enrichment.

Chapter Fourteen

Progress With That Scruffy Coat and PLEASE Tell Us What You Need, Mads!

Within the realms of safety, giving a dog a level of choice in how they spend their life: what they eat, when they eat, how they play, and who they interact with, is obviously conducive to how they feel, and is vital in enhancing their emotional wellbeing. In order to be able to hear and see what they're telling us, though, we need them to be tuned into us, and likewise, we need to be tuned into them – how are they really feeling? What indications are they giving us about how they feel about what is going on for them emotionally? With every other dog this had worked out very quickly, even with dog-aggressive Oskar and people-aggressive Charlie, but with Mads, his internal wall was consistently bouncing our attempted communications all over the place!

Despite our earlier recognition that he was finally making eye contact with us, there were times when he still wouldn't look at us; indeed, there were even times when I wondered whether he even realized we were there. He seemed to be utterly oblivious to our presence – I suppose I could describe him at that time as having been emotionally shut down.

While connecting with him was difficult, we slowly made inroads into certain aspects of what he was doing, and what he needed, in that we began to understand what we needed to do with him for him! It was one step forward and three steps back as we made tiny amounts of progress. After two months, house training was good 99% of the time.

Around that time, Mads would allow me to brush him, not just one leg or his neck, or one fluffy foot at a time, but we could have a good ten minutes a day, with treats, of course. I used to say to my students that the reason I had smooth coated dogs was because of the attention to their coats that longer coated dogs needed. Running a hound glove over a greyhound a few times a week was much quicker than the time intensity requirements of longer coated dogs.

After bringing Mads into our lives, in the coming months, we were to discover just how much care and attention was needed for a dog's coat that was as silky as a saluki and as fluffy as a collie. But by then I had retired from teaching and knew there'd be more time in the day to spend on brushing a dog's fur, as you really do need a lot of time set aside to prevent these long-coated dogs from becoming matted. And Mads would get muddy and scruffy in abundance and appeared to need more than one brush a day!

He was finally looking far more presentable than the What-a-Mess lookalike who had inhabited the house for the first few weeks. 'What-a-Mess' was a children's book character and TV series from the 1980s, and without a doubt, Mads featured the book's protagonist. He frequently sported twigs and leaves caught in his fur and would run around the garden like there was no tomorrow, caking himself in as much mud as he could. By three months, I was using brushing him as a way to calm him, because I'd realized as he began to push himself into the bristles, that he was actually enjoying the process.

His problem upon arrival, and for some time afterwards, was his fearfulness of being touched. He would cower away from our hands, whether we were attempting to fuss him, check him over, or brush him. He had clearly never known the joy that a gentle brush could offer him and the benefits to his health and hygiene. We wanted him to play in the garden, but we also desperately needed him to trust us enough to sort out the consequences of his having played outside: we had to sort out that mud which hardened on the fur between his toes, and sort out those mats which lodged themselves among the long tresses around his face, belly, and legs. And those sticks and leaves, my goodness, there were so many bits of nature twisted into his otherwise silky locks. He was such a scruffy dog.

Behaviourists will tell you to reward, reward, reward each small step – and it worked! Little by little, cleaning one toe at a time, one gentle brush along his back – not too much at once, one tiny, tiny step, always rewarded with treats. And then, oh so gradually, brushing his fur, giving him footbaths, cleaning his ears, giving worm pills, brushing his teeth, even clipping his toenails, all these things were accepted. I'm in no way suggesting he loved any of them, except for brushing, he really adored it and would let you brush his back and then he'd roll over and lie back in ecstasy as we brushed his chest, belly, his axillae ('armpits') and the inside of his hindlegs. And those mats and bits of the garden were teased out one by one.

On approach before we brushed him, we'd just say 'brush' to him, and show him the brush, at which, he relaxed back into the chair or cushion and seemed to love all the attention. He was such a stark contrast to the dog who at first would cower and try to escape from us whenever we attempted to get close to him.

While I brushed him, I would often think of some of the theory classes I used to teach about the benefits of grooming dogs, and how I used to reinforce that it was a way of helping someone to bond with their dog. I would smile to myself and wonder how much of a bore I would have been to the students had I not already been retired at that point in Mads' story! If I'd still been teaching, the classes would have been filled with tales of the antics of our new, unkempt, almost-feral dog.

Grooming is, indeed, a great way to bond with

dogs – once you can get them to accept you near to them, of course. While I'd introduced the brush to Mads gently and accompanied the brushing with treats, within a few months he needed no treats to be brushed, as the act of brushing was reward enough for him. Gentle brushing with the right equipment for the dog is such a companionable thing for both dog and person. Even old three-legged collie Charlie, while he hated baths (and no amount of his favourite treats would change that), quite enjoyed his fur being brushed, especially along his back and the front of his neck.

Grooming a dog is an opportunity to check a dog's overall health: to get those eyes, ears, teeth, nails, skin, and anogenital areas examined. And along the way while brushing Mads, I found old scars on his legs – most likely from him having got into scrapes while on the loose.

On discovering where the brush was stored, Mads would go and collect the brush for me and drop it at my feet; sometimes I'd find him chewing at the handle, and, as a consequence, we have a few chomped dog brushes that don't have an intact handle! In my mind he was bringing the brush to me because he liked being brushed, but probably in reality, he actually considered the brushes to be chew toys. He was also partial to chewing furniture and I had to reupholster his own sofa and a chair because of his early-on cheeky chewing habits.

As such an intelligent type of dog, collies have very special emotional needs and a desperately deep desire to be busy all the time. And it gradually dawned on us more and more that a major part of Mads' genetic make-up was, indeed, less hound and more collie. As a result of this, we came to understand that his whines, his barking, his need to be busy all the time, were all part of him and the genes that had mixed to create this perfectly imperfect hybrid. We had inadvertently brought another damaged, neurotic collie into our lives, and had to rewind all our expectations of living with another dog with a greyhound-like temperament. By comparison, greyhound types are generally much easier to understand; they're much more basic in their emotional ways. In accepting this change in our perception of him, we had to try to unravel whatever experiences he'd encountered that had made him the way he was, and respect that he was, indeed, more collie than hound.

Four months into our relationship with him, we still felt we hardly knew him. Likewise, he must have been utterly perplexed at all his interactions with humans. Despite the progress on the grooming front, I think he still wasn't sure whether we could be trusted. Because he couldn't tell us what he needed, to help him we instead needed to make certain assumptions about him and what he had been through, and use those assumptions to try to unravel his problems:

Assumption One: At some point, we don't know for sure when, because in reality he could have been any age from eighteen months to six years, he'd been a puppy who had been brought into a home and perhaps had even initially been loved.

Assumption Two: As he'd grown, his own needs hadn't been taken care of and, as a result, he'd developed behavioural problems.

Assumption Three: Because of this, he'd been beaten. This, we knew was a broad assumption which we didn't know for sure, however his fear response upon being approached and handled was like dogs I'd nursed years ago who had been hurt and had come from known, abusive human-dog relationships.

Assumption Four: He had also been shut in a cage. When he was at the rescue shelter, he had severe mental breakdowns whenever he was confined and had twice injured himself trying to escape.

Assumption Five: In his previous 'home' his behavioural problems did not improve (not surprisingly).

Assumption Six: Because of behavioural problems, he was turned out onto the streets to a fate which the previous people he lived with could not care less about. If he wasn't actually abandoned in such a way, then perhaps he escaped from somewhere, but even if that was the case, it was the local authority that picked him up and therefore he would not have been difficult to locate. Did he live or did he die? Presumably, those people (just as in the histories of Ralph and Charlie) have no idea whatsoever that he survived.

Assumption Seven: He spent some time on the streets, ducking and diving to survive. We know he was found on the streets, but we don't know how long he'd been there.

And then, of course, someone rescued him and took him to safety.

From that point on, we know for sure what happened. He spent the statutory week waiting in kennels to see whether he would be claimed – and then because the local authority he was found in had no space in their shelters, he was moved to our local rescue kennels.

These assumptions which we made enabled us to understand a little more about how to be around him:

We couldn't do very much about his puppyhood... all we know for sure is that at some point he was a puppy, of course he was, and the dog lottery dictated where he ended up. Puppies are sweet, they're adorable, and they usually bring out the best in people, but it was likely that wherever he ended up was not a suitable home for him.

By not taking care of his needs, whatever

happened to him established a path on which so many humans fail — and dogs suffer as a consequence of that failure. From his innate ducking and diving in those first few months with us, the assumption that he was previously hit by someone seems likely. Kicking, too, seems to have been something he'd endured because feet were also a huge problem with him. If we were sitting and one of us suddenly crossed our legs, he would cower as our foot was raised. He wouldn't shy away a little, but would fall to the floor in a defensive way — as though someone had made contact with him. This, of course, was something that never happened — he was safe with us, and we so wanted him to know that. And so, we were careful not to cross our legs when he was in the vicinity of our feet. Strangely, after about six months, one of his favourite places became lying on the rug with his head resting right on Connor's feet — healing really can happen, given time.

Mads revealed several 'skills' which indicated he probably had to fend for himself on the streets for some time. He appeared to know all about wheelie bins. When he first arrived, each Tuesday evening when all the bins were lined up like soldiers along the streets, as we walked along with him, he would jump up at them in an effort to knock them over or try to flip the lid. Bin lids and doors posed few problems for him. He didn't know door handles in the way that some incredibly clever dogs seem to, but he knew straight away that pushing a door would open it (while the other two watched in amazement at this entity who knew how to push a door). With kitchen bins, he knew immediately that by sticking his nose under the edge of the bin lid, the lid would come flying off and he could reach whatever was inside. Had severe hunger previously forced him to learn these behaviours?

He also obsessively foraged in dirt looking for bugs and worms. Only one other dog we've ever lived with has done that to the extent that he did, and that was Chip, who we knew for sure had existed for some time on the streets before being taken to an animal sanctuary in which I volunteered. She became my first very own dog who I was allowed to bring home from the animal sanctuary when I got my first veterinary nursing job and wasn't going to have so much time to volunteer there – she and I had bonded quickly after we met.

Another thing common to Chip and Mads (and, of course, Ralph), was that initial, distinct flight reaction to perceived threats – sometimes real, but mostly perceived. Yes, we and all other animals have fight, flight, freeze or fawn (appeasement) reactions, but with these particular three dogs, the flight reaction was much more pronounced. It was never fight, always an attempt to flee, whether the danger was real or perceived. Once caught (because sometimes circumstances mean you need to get them back to you – to clean ears etc., with rewards, of course) that's when the freeze, and sometimes fawn, reactions would happen. Fawn reactions resulted in them lip licking, crouching, having a tucked tail with perhaps apprehensive wagging, exposing their belly, and averting their gaze – all appeasement or subtle stress signs.

Knowing what he wanted from us was our priority, and as time went by his needs became more obvious, we were to be much more active. We had a relatively active routine with our middle-aged greyhound and elderly lurcher, however Mads had arrived in our lives and clearly needed more than they needed. The walks needed to be longer, running about outside had to last for much more time, and when not running or walking, he needed toys stuffed with food, snuffle mats, interesting chews, and regular recycling of toys and balls.

When he was resting but not sleeping (he rarely slept in those early times), had had lots of exercise and we were working nearby, we sometimes resorted to the mechanical babysitter and played episodes of dog rescue programmes, because we discovered he loved TV. While Ralph and Nell would occasionally respond to a sound emitting from the television, and Nell became a refined David Attenborough fan, Mads was quickly a canine documentary enthusiast. His favourite parts were when the dogs were playing with squeaky toys, and he would sit transfixed to the image on the screen, cocking his head at the sounds.

Our own learning curve was huge, and the learning curve of each of the dogs – about how to fit in with one another and how to be in their new way of being, was probably even greater. There was inevitably going to be some complex canine politics along the way!

Chapter Fifteen

Attempting to Understand the Dog Politics

In the time that followed Nell breaking the checkmate we had arrived at in trying to communicate with Mads, the two of them began to have a daily play, wrestling on the sitting room floor. Outside, too, they'd play together – when the weather was good anyway, as Nell had never really embraced bad weather. While there were times that I felt she was a bit rough with him, he seemed to enjoy the rough and tumble and rolled over on his back to let her wrap her jaws around his head. All the time, the two of them would be happily wagging their tails. She was very good at easing off him, however, if I told her she was being too rough. She was also very good at sharing toys with him (something we thought might be a problem, as she is very focused when she plays with toys), and we found balls to be a good distraction from them engaging in more physical play. She even let him take toys from her mouth, and she sometimes tossed them to him when she had finished playing with them.

Once Mads' recall was better and we no longer needed the long line for extra security, when outdoors playing fetch, Nell could mostly outrun him – she is a greyhound, after all – and catch the toy or ball. She sometimes ran off with it back into the house – these greyhounds really do like their comforts, and a lot of enthusiastic play is not always on the agenda. That's where Mads was different, and that genetic make-up I spoke of had created a dog who would keep on going and going for hours, only ever letting up to go and sniff around the entrances to the rabbit warren beside the sycamore tree. The rabbits had more sense, though, than to come out when their potential predators were on the prowl. Mads also developed a penchant for poking his face into any holes he found in the ground – always risking getting a nip on the nose from whatever creature had made their home there.

While Nell and Mads had their antics going on, Ralph meanwhile, liked to be quiet when the two of them were playfighting – his interactions with Mads were much gentler. There were times, however, when the athletic Mads would leap from the hall, over the sofa where Ralph was resting (sometimes over Ralph), and onto the living room floor, all in one swift move. There was a reason why the rescue shelter had named him Swift! And when they were outside and running around in 'zoomie' fashion, often with Ralph trailing along behind and joining in the fun from afar, it was an absolute joy.

Of course, Nell was the fastest, but her sidekick could nearly keep up with her, his flexible body enabling him to turn quickly and make a little ground on those corners, or when jumping over (or avoiding in Nell's case) the logs which were from trees cut down by the people who used to own our house. And then, worn out from their racing and sparring, they would rest, often sharing a bowl of cool water before they did. There were several bowls around, but they always went to the same one – there was some level of innate bonding going on after each run around.

I'd heard of dogs who'd been rescued from abroad, or dogs who had, like Mads, spent time living on the streets, that when they first arrived, they sometimes wouldn't initially appreciate the creature comforts on offer to them. Many of them would rather go and lie on a rug on the hard kitchen floor instead of on the cozy bed and sofa that they could lie on. Mads was no different, and as we humans and canines assembled to sit and eat or watch a film, Mads would lie in an adjoining room staring at us all through the doorway. It worried me – would he ever feel a part of the family?

Gradually, however, he watched and learned, and I suppose he saw where Ralph and Nell rested and thought, 'Hey, why not?' And so, while he did continue for about the first six months or so to sometimes go and lie down on his own on the hard floor, it became less frequent. I suppose it came back to that whole 'choice' factor previously discussed – he could choose what he preferred to do, and in that time, that place, he was more comfortable maintaining a bit of distance between himself and the humans he felt he could not yet trust.

Whenever he did it, we'd place a soft dog bed pad next to him to try to get him to lie on that instead, but often he'd simply just lay on the rug, watching us all from that safe distance and taking everything in. We watched him back and tried to encourage him through to us, meanwhile imagining his brain ticking over as he seemed to be calculating a risk: benefit factor. Ralph and Nell must have considered him to be just a little odd – after all, why would anyone lie on a hard floor if a comfier place was available?

When teaching animal care subjects, I used to say that beanbags were nice and comfortable (for non-chewing dogs, of course), but not so suitable for old dogs as they have difficulty getting on and off them. Not geriatric Ralph, though! Over the years he had become a class act at navigating the contours of a beanbag and no old age symptoms were going to stop him. And from the side-lines, Mads watched. He eventually developed his own manner of negotiating his way around a beanbag, which wasn't very graceful. He would invariably be found lying half-on, half-off, with head and rib cage in contact with the bag, and his hindlegs draped across the carpet. He began to take his food-stuffed toys there too, much to my distaste as I imagined much more frequent washing of the beanbag cover, and with that, those associated polystyrene beads being scattered all over the floor.

And so, things were going okay – brilliantly, in

fact – but there was an unexpected turn in events to come. I'm not even sure I'll ever understand why things took such a big change in how the dogs became with each other. Their subtle signs are often beyond the true interpretation of we mere humans, and whatever happened between Nell and Mads was to hold back any progress they'd made for many months – to the extent that we wondered whether they would ever again be properly okay with each other.

We noticed a change in how they were with each other when they were running around the BG. His teasing of her had become more frequent; her chasing him more intense. Instead of sparring with him when she caught up with him, she was leaping on top of him and grabbing him by the neck. While he thought it was a big game, it didn't seem that way to us humans who were watching from the side-lines.

After it had happened a few times, we decided to intervene. They remained absolutely fine with one another in the house, on walks, and in the garden behind the house. The tension only ever built up in the BG when Mads got over-excited, and when Nell forgot she was no longer running around a track chasing a mechanical hare. The speed they could reach out there also seemed to be a factor.

It was strange, because those were the fears I'd had with Peggy and little Lucy, as Lucy was far more rabbit-like and rabbit-sized, but Peggy was always fine with Lucy (once she acknowledged she was a dog!). With Nell and Mads, though, his similarity to a rabbit or hare was only that he was mostly brown. Oh, and of course, he could run fast and duck and swerve in the same way a canid's prey would.

We realized we had to be careful! New rules had to be put into place for whenever we were in the BG, and we decided that only one of them would be able to run free with Ralph at a time when they were all out there together. While one of them was playing (either with or without Ralph, depending on his level of playfulness at the time) with a ball or toy, the other would be mooching about on a lead having a sensory, snuffle walk with one of us and receiving treats. And doing this seemed to restore peace.

On hot days when no one was wanting to run around anyway, they were able to both be off the lead, and we started allowing them to run to the gate between the two gardens together once playtime was over and there was the promise of treats awaiting in the house (that word 'biscuit' is so very powerful).

Treats while we were out there, too, were coming in handy, especially as Nell, like most greyhounds, is incredibly food motivated! We constantly rewarded her for being calm around him when he was running, and rewarded him for being calm around her and not going and jumping about in front of her face to torment her. And it helped, especially as they seemed to get the message: absolutely no dancing around by Mads in front of Nell's nose, and no chasing and grabbing a hold of Mads by Nell!

A greyhound is a strange creature, though, and it's not surprising when we consider the life they've come from. As sighthound (and greyhounds in particular) guardians, we face a huge battle when they come to us because they have often endured so much in their time as racing dogs that they are emotionally broken. Lurchers and other sighthounds may have experienced abuse as well if they've been used as hunting dogs.

And then, carefully, slowly, we have to gain their trust and fix them all one small piece at a time. After all, these sometimes-aloof hounds are the gentle ones – unassuming and happy just to be, but these so-called 'sports' continue with little or no concern for the dogs involved.

Chapter Sixteen

Being Sighthound Guardians

In the past, I've written and spoken a lot about greyhounds. I would talk a lot about them when I was teaching. Students contribute to that, too, they find something you love and ask you a question during a lecture on an otherwise boring subject, knowing it will distract you for a bit. With the engineers at work, I heard that their students would deliberately ask questions about Land Rovers for the same reason.

To all my ex-students, especially the cat-obsessed ones, I apologize for my slight obsession with all dogs, but particularly greyhounds and lurchers. I don't claim to be a greyhound expert and have only ever shared my life with two – many lurchers, but only two greyhounds. Some people I know have many rescued greyhounds, and they, I am sure, would be able to talk from now until the end of time about their love of these elegant, gentle dogs.

In countries across the world where greyhound racing is seen as a sport, greyhounds who don't make the grade will suffer. Even those who are successful in the eyes of the trainers and owners, will be cast aside or used for breeding once their running days are over. If used for breeding, once those days are done and they are no longer being productive, they, too, will be pushed aside – to goodness knows what kind of fate. Their lives are mostly in barren kennel blocks, sometimes with greyhounds for company, but if kept in single kennels, they don't even have that companionship.

Without the support of individuals, for it is gamblers and their addiction that keep the industry going, greyhound racing would not exist. It is big money for the trainers, the track owners, bookies, and the television stations that screen the races. The gambler, however, is often the vulnerable person in the middle of it all; they're the person who lives for the short, sharp thrill of the race. And many races can be squeezed into an afternoon on the track, and much money is lost. Therein lies the social problem, but the dogs — the dogs lose all the time. They're at the bottom of the greyhound racing pecking order; they are born into a life where their existence depends on being successful. After racing is done, the luckier ones will be handed to a charity who will take care of them until they can find a loving home. Not all race trainers hand their 'waste' dogs over to shelters, and some of those dogs meet an incredibly unfortunate end.

The long-term effects of racing injuries are rarely spoken about. Our old Peggy had severe pain because of the injuries she sustained on the track, and for all her time with us (from the age of four), she had to be on pain relief. As she got older, her medication had to be increased to allow for the pain which had begun breaking through. In the end, it was her severe levels of pain, coupled with her frequent collapsing and being unable to get up, which forced us to have her euthanized. It was heart-breaking to think that her life was shortened because of her having been used as a racing dog.

You see old dogs with wheels, but in a big, old dog is that ethical? She used to scream in pain when she stumbled, and that is no life for a dog. It was her hips and one of her shoulders that hurt, and pain relief was no longer effective in the places where she needed it. Attaching a set of wheels to her would have been impossible and something, given her degree of pain, we never considered. We were heartbroken that we could no longer help our beautiful, yipping, demanding girl. We'd been defeated by the people who made money from breeding and racing her.

If Nell runs around too much then she wants to rest for a while afterwards, but we can't find any obvious sign of injury in her, we're never really sure if her lack of interest in running is simply her being a greyhound, or whether there might be some underlying pain from an old injury, in a location we haven't yet identified. She certainly doesn't have the stamina of energetic Mads, but she's a few years older, and greyhounds are notorious for being sofa-dwelling creatures. A short run, and they're often done for the day and, apart from a couple of strolls, will often spend the rest of the day lying contentedly on their backs – roaching, as it's more commonly known (which is a little confusing, as in modern times this term has been applied to someone who dates and sees a lot of people without telling a new partner – language is such a mysterious thing).

I long so much for a worldwide end to greyhound racing; this has been a wish for a very long time. Will it ever end? I imagine only with much government backing. Why do we have to fight for what the majority of people know is right? In America, dog racing is now illegal in forty-two states. As I write this, in Scotland we are hopeful of a ban being imminent. I hope that we will soon see this ground-breaking change, for it is an incredibly cruel sport, through both intentional harm and neglect. A ban in Scotland will hopefully influence other UK nations to follow suit.

Meanwhile, there is no doubt that across the world thousands of dogs suffer, and I hope if Scottish legislation is enacted that they will also introduce a ban on the export of dogs for racing. Many greyhounds fall by the wayside – never registered and simply disappearing. Greyhounds were once often found dead with their ears cut off to remove their tattoos, this was more common before mandatory microchipping, with it increasing traceability. Even with mandatory microchipping for dogs, many still turn up in rescue without a chip, so along the way the system is not being properly enforced.

Finding Nell and Mads

And so, the dogs who are lucky enough to find themselves in rescue will hopefully find a forever home. Once they're there, there is something greyhound guardians will discover: greyhounds are not really like other dogs!

I suppose you could say that about any breed, in that collies, retrievers, Chihuahuas, Yorkshire terriers, mastiffs, and so on, are all very different to one another, and have their own traits. But there really is something about having a greyhound about the place which is quite different. And both Peggy and Nell brought with them interesting characteristics.

There's a gentleness about greyhounds which you do see in other large hounds, such as borzois or deerhounds. It's a gentleness which appears to extend to concern – especially concern about themselves – there's a lot of so-called navel-gazing in these hounds. They ponder away to themselves and appear to be contemplating what's happening in the present and even, perhaps, reflecting on what has happened in the past.

Greyhounds avidly watch you. This may be for treats (it is, indeed, often for treats), but they seem to need to know what you are doing... all the time. By comparison, at first Mads had little interest in us, and would only pay attention if it was a part of his routine and he was waiting for the next thing to tick off his list of things which he came to know would happen every day, the rest of the time he'd do his own thing. As our worlds became integrated, though, that changed. I'm not sure when or how it happened, but his interest in us grew so much that it became greater even than Nell's.

Nell would always do the ticking things off a list thing too, but in a more nuanced way. Our old Peggy used to stand in front of us and emit her screech-like bark until we did whatever she wanted us to do, which wasn't the easiest if we were not quite sure what she was after (those treats, no doubt). Her piercing bark was something else.

By comparison, Nell has quite a gruff voice. Her muscles were abnormally and unnaturally large when she came to us. Over time, her muscle mass became much more normal, but her gruff bark remained. Her weight was interesting too, at about the same height as Peggy, on arrival she was a good eight kilos heavier – and Peggy was longer. Peggy had a good body condition score, and so did Nell. Those huge muscles just made her look out of proportion. The nurses at the vet clinic commented on her huge 'wiggle bottom' the first time they met her.

The trait which is unbelievably common to all these dogs, however, is the one which gives them their characteristic description as being sighthounds. A sighthound's eyes are on the front of their skull. If they have their head pointing in a particular direction, they won't miss a thing from where they are standing and out as far as the horizon. This is great, until you are on the other end of a lead and a small dog, a cat, a rabbit, a rodent, a soft toy, even a fly, is in their line of sight. In the early days, Nell's thirty-eight kilo body weight was a force to be reckoned with when I was walking her, and she spotted something in the distance before I could distract her with treats.

Many moons ago, we were dog-sitting for friends for a couple of weeks. Their dog was a huge lurcher named Berek. He was an amazingly, lovable, crossed wolfhound/deerhound, or perhaps another large dog in there too. He was the gentlest, kindest large dog you could hope to meet. One day we were out for our regular walk with him and our other two dogs of the time – Chip the building site dog and Fluke the collie cross. Connor was still very young, probably about four or five, and I was walking along holding his hand and had our two dogs' leads in the other hand. Alun was holding onto Berek.

So, along we strolled, chattering away, but then, unbeknownst to Alun, Berek spotted a cat. Now, we knew that Berek had a thing about cats, but never before, or since, have I seen any dog and human combination move so fast. They were beside Connor and me, but then in the blink of an eye, they were at the back gate of someone's house. Berek was jumping up and clearly trying to clear the gate, while Alun was holding on tight, attempting not to be dragged over said gate with Berek. The cat, thankfully, had escaped over the fence and probably scaled several fences in fear for his life. Which, I suppose, brings me onto the next trait sight hound guardians need to be aware of, and that's speed!

They are fast! Most hounds are obviously known for their speed; they have been bred that way – and greyhounds can reach speeds of almost forty-five miles per hour. The cheetah is faster (at about seventy-five miles per hour), but the greyhound is particularly good at sustaining their speed over relatively longer distances. Their gallop is a graceful one, if a little terrifying if they're heading towards you. I've learned that the best tactic for avoiding collision is just to stand still – they really have seen you and will whoosh past you (in most cases anyway), and you'll feel the gust of wind as they do!

Wherever there are racing dogs or sighthounds being used for hunting, you'll generally find rescue charities will be working nearby, gathering the dogs from the streets, or waiting for people to hand the dogs in. In Spain there are the Galgos, the Spanish greyhounds. They're very much like the greyhounds found elsewhere, but are generally finer, with a more streamlined musculature than their regular greyhound counterparts. Like lurchers, they are generally used for hunting, but then, once the hunting season is done, many of the dogs are cast aside

– left to fend for themselves, and some are tortured. It's so very sad that for their speed, slender hounds are persecuted.

The original lurchers were crossed collie-greyhounds. Collies for their endurance and intelligence, and greyhounds for their speed. As years have passed, the lurcher is now seen as being any large, crossed sighthound, or crossed whippet, for that matter.

With deerhounds and wolfhounds, while also sighthounds, their fate has somehow not resulted in them being persecuted in quite the same way... you see crosses which have that distinctive rough coat and may be bred for coursing, but for the most part, the purebred dogs appear to have been protected from the experiences many of their hound cousins have had to endure. Except historically, perhaps, a dog known as Gelert:

Some may be familiar with Gelert's story. I remember my whole school being told about him in a morning assembly. The story goes that Gelert was the dog of the Prince Llywelyn, and the tale of this loyal dog brings with it a strong message:

It was said that in the 1200s, the Prince Llywelyn went off to hunt with his pack of hounds. On return, he realized that the dog Gelert had not joined him. He then spotted the dog with blood around his mouth and immediately assumed Gelert had killed his baby son. The prince immediately drove a sword through the heart of the dog and killed him.

It is said that Llewellyn then heard the cry of his baby. He rushed to see him and found, beside his son's cradle, a dead wolf. The message coming through strong and clear in that assembly when I was perhaps eleven or twelve, was to never jump to conclusions. The story ended with the head teacher telling us that the prince never smiled again. For years, that story haunted me.

We visited the grave of Gelert – it's in a place in Wales called Beddgelert, which means 'grave of Gelert.' It transpires, however, that unfortunately the stones that form the grave were put there by a businessman who owned the local public house in the late 1700s. And so, unlike the much more well-known (and true) Edinburgh story of Greyfriar's Bobby, the story of Gelert is said to be a folk tale concocted by the publican named Pritchard!

Before the Welsh Tourist Board comes after me, it's worth adding that Beddgelert is in the beautiful Snowdonia National Park and is well worth a visit to bask in the mountain air and view the astounding scenery. It is even worth visiting that grave of Gelert, because you never know, the old tale could be true! Even in summer it's cold in those hills, though, so remember to pack a coat for your delicate greyhound.

While I don't agree with dressing dogs up for the sake of it (let dogs be dogs), greyhounds have come a long way from their wild origins and need a coat... this is essential dog wear for greyhounds and any dog with similar fur. Without a coat on, they will get extremely cold, and stand trembling and looking up at you sorrowfully whenever you stop walking. Nell has the most amazing Arctic-quality, bright pink coat, but even that doesn't take into account her sparsely covered chest and belly. Greyhounds (just like Staffordshire terriers, Dobermanns, and similar-coated dogs) have very short fur which doesn't have an undercoat, which many dogs have which helps to keep them warm.

Taking all this into account – history and traits combined, anyone would be privileged to have a greyhound in their life – they really are something special. I perhaps sound like someone who loves a breed or type of dog, rather than all dogs. There are people who like a particular breed and won't ever deviate from that type of dog, whereas I really do passionately love all dogs, whatever they look like – all animals, for that matter.

I think with us, that we see that these bigger hound types are harder to rehome than some of the smaller lap dogs or dogs with squashed faces (brachycephalic dogs) and I suppose over time we've become accustomed to their ways. I would happily have a little dog live with us, but like most people, we must draw the line somewhere. In our case, while I know that three dogs are our maximum, it would be wonderful to be able to give a home to many more.

Perhaps when I'm old and grey (the grey is increasing almost by the day) a little dog will make their way into our lives again – another dog like our old little (twelve kilogram) Lucy would be perfect. Just like all the other dogs gone by, she enhanced our world for the time we had her here with us. I do miss her little-dog ways and hope we were worthy of her reciprocal affection.

Chapter Seventeen

Some Rescue Dogs Gone By

Do dogs compare what they have now with what their life was before? This thought has occurred to me many times over the years when I see dogs who were previously abandoned snuggling down into their comfortable bed, or happily playing fetch in the garden.

People say that dogs live in the moment, but both Ralph and Mads have shown quite clearly that there are residual thoughts and feelings which are difficult to overcome. Their initial fears of us and their expectation that something bad would happen to them if they approached us, surely that demonstrates that perhaps (as many think) they have few thoughts of the future beyond their next meal or next walk, for instance, but their past is forever with them. Truly living in the moment would mean there was no residual fear that their actions may have dire consequences for them.

What does it take for someone to turn a dog out on the streets, to drive them miles away so they can't find their way home, leaving them to the lap of the gods? If people are not coping, there is a rescue shelter or two in every town, and even though they may not be able to take the dog immediately, they will often do so as quickly as they can. Many years ago, someone I knew told me a story of someone who, a few years earlier, had taken their Labrador from their town to the next, stopped there, opened the car door, pushed the dog out, and driven off. What possesses people to do such a thing? It sickens me to think about it – the dog was apparently caught by the dog warden and taken to a shelter, so hopefully his ending was a happy one.

When he was found as a young dog, collie Charlie had had exactly the same thing happen, only the people first bound his legs together. His legs were covered in deep grazes on the undersides, and where they had bound his legs, the ropes had dug into his paws. Beyond that, like Mads, he had been starved, and his ribs, spine, and the tops of his hips were clearly visible underneath his skin. A dog's body shape is scored on a scale of 1-9, with 1-3 being too thin, 4-5 being of an ideal weight, 6 is the shape of dogs who are struggling with their weight and said to be above ideal, 7 is the overweight dogs, and 8 and 9 are those dogs who are obese. On this now well-recognized scale, when he arrived with us, Charlie was absolutely a 1; skinny Mads was a 2-3. I imagine when he had arrived at the kennels his body score would have been a 2.

When working in animal shelters, I nursed many thin and undernourished dogs, and it was the most rewarding thing to see them gradually put on weight. Their fur would begin to shine from them finally getting the right nutrients, their energy levels would increase, and their personality would emerge. All these benefits to the dog from finally receiving food and water! That all-important full belly is such a basic need, and one which no dog should be denied.

When dogs are very underweight, like Mads was, they need six small meals a day. The temptation would be to fill them up straight away with huge bowls of food, but suddenly getting diarrhoea would not be conducive to their healing. And so, with Mads, because he'd already been nursed by the kennels staff, we continued with his intensive feeding care. And little by little, those ribs, tops of hips and vertebrae became less palpable and then less visible under his skin. As that happened, his fur became glossier, and his muscles filled out.

We can do that with food, we can make their body score improve. What we can't do, however, is take away the mental scarring that arises from being mistreated. Do we know for sure that this happened to Mads (or Ralph and Charlie, for that matter)? Of course, we don't, but there are behavioural reactions which tell a story, and that story is the one which you perceive to be the truth. We can see their reactions and surmise that if we move our foot over to cross our legs when we're sitting down, and the dog cowers, they are nervous of human feet – and something bad probably happened to cause that fear. Likewise, if we reach out to them and they recoil away from us, there is something deeply embedded in their psyche which must be resolved, and their response changed to one of trust.

Most dogs have fur, and their fur conceals bruising, meaning physical mistreatment would often go unrecognized and therefore unreported to relevant charities or the police, unless someone actually witnesses it happening. Even for the lucky ones who get rescued, those mental scars linger; meanwhile, you try to let the dog know that they are safe now, and everything will be all right.

It took months of nursing Charlie the collie at home to get him back to health, and then my brother Mark adopted him. For ten years he lived with Mark, and he had a lot of canine friends on his long walks over to see Mum (dogs were never his problem, just people, and not surprisingly). Mum always had a dog – for most of that time another collie, Gail, who became Charlie's best dog buddy. Charlie was a naughty dog and did that thing that collies sometimes do, whereby he used to nip. You had to be careful not to crouch down or lean forward when he was around as he was particularly partial to nipping bottoms. But despite this, we all loved him.

Charlie unfortunately also had another trait which is very much collie-related, in that whenever a car went by, he would throw himself down on the path to intently watch it and bark at it. Sadly, this eventually resulted in a stress fracture of his elbow. The elbow was operated on and repaired, but the fracture broke again. The injury had involved the muscle coming away from his bone, bringing with it a small piece of that bone. While it was screwed back in place, it was quite a vulnerable fracture repair and, because of its location, when it broke again it became inoperable. At this point, Charlie had gained a few excess pounds, which hadn't helped with his car-related antics. And so, his leg was removed.

When Charlie lost his leg, it was difficult for my brother to keep him because by then he couldn't walk so well himself and he was on kidney dialysis, and so we had Charlie live with us for the last couple of years of his life. We managed very quickly to get him to lose the pounds, simply by putting him on a high fibre diet which filled him up without the calories, and luckily Charlie liked carrots – all that generation of dogs did. Right from the start, Ralph and Mads looked at me as though I had three heads if I offered them a carrot. Nell used to as well, but over time she became partial to the odd crunch away at one! Mads and Ralph protested by chomping them into the tiniest pieces and then spitting them over their beds or the sofa – with all the enthusiasm they could muster!

Charlie coped well as a three-legged dog, and he could easily keep up with Oskar and Dillon as we walked along the cycle paths and through the forests. Charlie would hop along beside his friend Dillon, while Oskar would always be on a lead as we could never trust him off lead with small dogs. I would take Charlie with me so he could visit Mark, Mum, and of course Gail, his best friend; in turn, they would come to visit him. The continuation of those friendships was vital for everyone – humans and dog buddies alike.

And then, a couple of years later and by then a very old dog, Charlie could no longer cope on his three legs when the other legs had become very arthritic, and we agreed with the vets that it was time to let him go. Like our other previous dogs, Charlie was put to sleep at home, after having been given a sedative to calm him – the last thing we wanted was for him to be stressed. This aged, cantankerous, bottom-nipping, but lovable collie passed away being held gently by people who loved him dearly. The people who had him previously had no idea of what became of him – he could have died in a gutter all those years before with his legs bound together and I'm sure they wouldn't have cared less.

Rescue dogs all bring with them a tale... some a tale of having loved and lost; others a tale of never having been loved at all. Some dogs, like Charlie, Ralph, and Mads come to you with no history whatsoever, especially if, like those three, they were taken in as strays. This results in there being no obvious indication of what they've endured and where they came from, except through their actions and responses to you.

Jack, too, was found as a stray and handed in to our local kennels. He was jet black with the most beautiful, kindest expression on his face. I loved him so very much. He would lie next to me on the bed each night, and he did that for all the time we were together, including through the year in which I had a dialysis machine at home, and I had to dialyze through the night. He was the gentlest of dogs, and I've written about him and told people many times that if there really is one dog in the world who steals your heart, if there really is that one perfect dog, then that was Jack. Once he died, I never used a picture of him in any of my lectures; I could never bring myself to, because I knew I would cry. On reflection, that is so very sad, for all the beautiful stories I had of him and which, in hindsight, I would love to have shared.

Some students met Jack in the early days of my teaching when I would take him into the classroom. It feels so long ago! It was back in the long-lost, nostalgic days of chalkboards and chalk. As the class was settling down, he would sometimes grab everyone's attention by stealing the chalk from in front of the board and running around the classroom with it. One day, as I picked up a piece of chalk from the teacher's table at the front of the class, I noticed there was something written on it! One of the students had written 'Jack's Sweetie' on the edge. I laughed so much. Those were the days of teaching when everything was so very light-hearted, a time when we would successfully get through our curriculum and have time for fun end of term quizzes.

In the years before I left, the pace of life and expectations of how much could be fitted into a day had changed, amid an increased workload and all the stresses that are involved with that. What did that? Was it computers and the demands they bring with the immediacy of emails? I'm only glad I had that time when my dogs could be in the classroom with me, and my colleagues could do the same with their dogs. I'm sure the students benefited from having them there too – except for the occasional classroom distraction induced by a chalk-stealing lurcher named Jack! Distraction aside, he would settle down quickly and would wait patiently for each break time.

Jack left us far too soon when he was only ten. We had packed so much joy into the years when he was with us, but when he developed breathing problems due to an inoperable mass in his nasal cavity, within weeks of that diagnosis, we had to say farewell to him.

Fluke, too, arrived as a stray. He was Jack's almost life-long buddy. He came into a charity where I was working as a veterinary nurse. We had no history on him, and he was brought in one evening when I was on duty. Despite his dislocated hip, as I booked him in, he stood in front of me wagging his tail. Realizing there was something wrong with his hindquarters, I called the vet to come and examine him. Not unlike Mads in appearance, he was a black and brindle collie-type but with a sleek, dark black on his back and brindle everywhere else coat (Mads is a lighter brindle with less black).

Fluke was a good dog and I feel sure someone somewhere had lost him, but not known how to find him. Or perhaps they had died, and someone turned him onto the streets. Whatever his mysterious origins, he arrived with his hip injury which was most likely from having been hit by a vehicle. While his hip joint was repaired, that joint was never very good, and he spent the final ten years or so of his life on pain relief. He was a great dogs' dog, but also loved people; we were incredibly lucky to have him in our lives.

I mentioned Chip before, who was my first very own dog. She was a strange dog, who I think now with all the years of living with other dogs, working with dogs, and teaching about dogs, I would understand better. On the building site on which she'd been found, she had proven incredibly difficult to catch. Youths had been seen throwing bricks at her, which had made her even more frightened of people. Eventually, after a few weeks of her periodically evading the dog warden on their mission to round up strays, one of the builders who was working there managed to persevere and catch her, despite her dodging him on many occasions. He'd

Finding Nell and Mads

gained her trust by feeding her chips, hence her name.

By the time I met her, she had already been at the animal sanctuary for more than two years and she'd overcome some of the fears she had when she arrived there, but she was still rather terrified of visitors to the sanctuary. When people came to offer dogs a home, she would follow them around and bark at them – she wasn't really selling herself very well, and back in those days, sanctuaries did little in the way of training to enable a dog to be more likely to find a home. And so, she became one of the sanctuary's residents. That was, until the day she and I met, and I fell in love with her.

She was incredibly dirty when we brought her home, so the first thing we did was to rush her to the bathroom and shower her in the bath. She was infested with fleas. I have never seen so much staining of digested blood from flea dirt on a dog's coat quite as memorably as I did that day. We rinsed her and rinsed her, and that digested blood from the flea dirt kept on staining her coat. How she wasn't anaemic, I'll never know. It appeared that in rescue shelters in those days, just as there was a lack of behavioural support for the dogs, parasite control wasn't much of a thing either.

As dogs do, Chip saw me through some of the toughest times, but also the best times, including Connor's birth. She was the gentlest soul and eventually overcame her fears of people, forgiving our species for the cruelty she had endured on that building site. I would go as far as to say that she became quite cheeky, in the best sense of the word. She was the dog who was perhaps most like Ralph, not only in colour, but also temperament.

What is it in our society that has been missed in terms of nurturing and education? I suppose people would say, 'Ah, yes, but people are cruel to people too, so we need to get that sorted out first.' But why must it be that way? Surely kindness should be the most important and integral part of how we behave and interact with others, no matter whether they are people, dogs, cats, cows, pigs, or the bird who flutters down to feed in your garden. Violence is violence, no matter on whom that violence is inflicted. By educating and nurturing, we can aim to eliminate violence for a more peaceful world for people and animals.

One dog we know for sure had been loved before was Dillon, and between him and other rescue dogs we've known, there was a profound, positive difference in attitude to life and how he interacted with everyone. He had so clearly never had hurt inflicted on him. The people he lived with before had been broken-hearted about having to let him go because of circumstances that were out of their control. I hope they got some comfort when they discovered he was adopted by a family (us) who at the time volunteered at the kennels. He and Connor were perfect companions.

Education about looking after dogs, and how to be around them, has improved greatly during the first two decades of this century. In the 1990s, we began to see a change in people's appreciation of dog behaviour, but now so much is understood about dogs, that with advice, people are better equipped to work through the problems. There are behaviourists and animal welfare organizations out there who all have dogs' best interests at heart and will help if they can. Prior to that, there was nothing like the level of advice, knowledge, and support available, and consequently many dogs were euthanized.

And so, those old ex-stray dogs, and many others who shared our lives, eventually led to this new team of three:

Ralph: the elderly, but still incredibly spritely, gentleman.

Nell: the long suffering 'mother' of the other two.

Mads: the troubled teenager with a big heart and a tendency towards being a hooligan.

Chapter Eighteen
Ralph, Nell, and Mads – the New Team of Three

Our old dog Peggy had taken good care of Ralph; Lucy had too, in her tiny, tearaway terrier way. When we brought Nell home to be Ralph's companion, we had no idea how their relationship would pan out in the long run. They'd had that shaky start when Nell had been bashing about in her Elizabethan cone and flinging her bandaged tail at him. But dogs never fail to surprise me, and while Peggy had watched over Ralph, Nell has mothered him. We've seen a side to her which in the early days we never thought we would see, as she is such a bold dog, but there is a gentleness to her character which she has since demonstrated time and time again.

Before Mads arrived, Nell and Ralph had developed a deep affection for one another – and she would often lie snuggled up to him with her head draped over his back, or occasionally he'd rest his over hers. They loved to reach out and touch one another with their toes and clearly felt great comfort in one another's company. Their deep affection for each other was such that, for Mads it was difficult to break through that bond, and for them to spare him a little of their inner circle, mutual caring.

Gradually, though, he went from being an outcast, ragamuffin, degenerate rascal from the streets, who Ralph and Nell's people suddenly enforced upon them, to being a dog they have taken under their elder wings.

These days, when I see the three of them together, it's as though they were always meant to be this band of three. They are a group of dogs who have all known the worst of society, have all been through hardship, but who have ended up inhabiting our sofas and every waking moment of our lives.

Even when we are asleep, they are there, dwelling in our dreams. I have a recurring nightmare of chasing Ralph along a busy road. It happened once when he was newly in our lives, and I've never got over that fear I had then that I would never see him again. Because he sleeps in his bed right next to me, I feel such a relief when I wake and peer over the edge of the bed and see his relaxed, snoozing body, safe and sound where no one can hurt him.

Now, it seems, Mads has begun to inhabit my dreams in a similar way, and in those dreams, I am chasing him along the busy road which bisects our village. In the dream, at the end of the village he stops and looks back at me, and I'm not sure, but I think he returns to me. The dream, however, has never reached the point where I actually have contact with him and can feel his fur. Is that even a thing? Can we reach out and touch in our sleep and truly feel the sensation of what we are touching?

And so, dogs, everyone loves dogs, right? And

our feline friends, too, of course? When I was still teaching, when teaching about animals and society, I would occasionally for fun do a short group task, whereby some groups would talk about the advantages and disadvantages of living with dogs, and the other groups the advantages and disadvantages of living with cats. This task would always bring out the best, wonderful things about sharing our lives with these species, along with the awful things we tolerate because we love them (such as dogs licking their bottoms in public and cats drooling over you while you stroke them).

Only, it seemed that one group was struggling – the group of six or seven of them couldn't think of one advantage of living with cats; they all hated them – with a passion! Short of asking them whether they were on the wrong course, and with my mouth agape (and the mouths of many of those in the other groups doing the task, equally agape), they went on to explain that none of them had any intention of working with cats – just dogs, horses, wild animals, or exotics. Absolutely, definitely, no cats.

How did that happen through a random selection of six or seven students from the group, all of them on an animal care course, that they could all be so anti-cat? I have never seen such a long list of negative reasons to not live with cats. They included: killing wild creatures, bringing said creatures to you, scratching you, demanding food (their piercing meow), wailing, litter trays, bossing other animals around by swiping at them, swiping at the hands that feed them even, scratching furniture, and so on, for what seemed like an endless list... this group could think of no benefits whatsoever of sharing our lives with our feline friends.

Those who preferred cats to dogs, but liked both, were horrified, as was I, as one who prefers dogs, but likes cats, which, to be honest, was the general consensus of the class. Just a couple of students in the class said they weren't so keen on dogs or cats and were doing the course to work with wildlife.

But dogs, too, have their moments! With all the love we have for them, dogs have some incredibly disgusting habits – and these three are no exception, especially the lovable rogue, Mads. You accept rescue dogs as they are, and hope that in time their bad habits will become less frequent. Dogs who have been left to live on the streets have to compete to survive. They must somehow find food by begging from people they come across, stealing it, or by exhibiting disgusting behaviours such as eating faeces.

But with all their issues, when you take on a dog, you agree to love them unconditionally... they may take over your life, but that's what it's about, isn't it? Whoever you are, and however you are with them, they love you back unconditionally. We should never take that adulation for granted and we owe it to them to give them the best life possible, so they are, indeed, '#livingtheirbestlife'!

As we came to know him better, it became apparent that Mads was the scruffiest, most mud-loving dog we'd ever lived with. While Nell had always daintily trotted around the gardens, with few bursts of energy and mostly keeping to the paths, Mads would throw himself around in the mud, sometimes diving into it and rubbing himself along. He'd get up, shake himself down and then throw himself in the pond for a splash about in the water – even on cold winter's days when the water was freezing cold.

Ralph, we noticed, unfortunately decided to take a leaf out of Mads' book, and while he didn't throw himself down in the mud, he scampered about in the muddy grass like he was a puppy seeing the world for the first time. Once caked in what looked like clay, at the back door the two of them would have to have their feet and bellies sponged down when they came back into the house; meanwhile Nell would stand by and watch in her superior queen-like, greyhound way. If shaking her head in a disappointed manner was in the greyhound behavioural repertoire, I'm sure she would have done that, as she stood by each day watching the two of them having their post-mud-bath wash.

Through all these years, the dogs we have taken into our hearts and our homes have often been tainted by the treatment they've had before, but for the most part, their resilience has helped them to recover. And along the way, there may have been a bit of chewing of furniture, the odd toileting accident in the house, and a bit of barking until they got used to everyone's routines. And even once all those things had settled down, our carpets would still get messed up with muddy pawprints, there would still be fur everywhere, they would smell from time to time, and as a result, we would end up with an unavoidable doggy smell in the house. And then, of course, there's occasionally dog vomit to deal with! But all these things are part of sharing our lives with dogs. Dogs absolutely give so much more than we offer them, and we humans often don't deserve their devotion.

Dogs surprise you sometimes with their agility and on one particularly sunny day we were in the garden with the three dogs for their afternoon run around. We know we are lucky to have a garden which is big enough for them to have a good gallop – we really did prioritize garden over house when we bought this cottage. Nell came outside for a little while, but after a short sniff about, seemed to decide that despite it being sunny, the day was too wet and cold for a greyhound. Her enthusiasm for being chased by Mads on this particular day was also not great, and she wandered back to the house and the comfort of a sofa – her sofa apparently. My brother refers to her as a 'greyhound-shaped cushion' (and he's not wrong). Without the short-sharp-burst Nell to chase, Mads and Ralph were thus left to do their own thing, at which, the then thirteen-year-old Ralph decided that that particular day was, indeed, a play day and a little interaction with Mads would be on the cards. And so, they played.

While Ralph played nicely with Mads, we watched with great pride as Mads neatly jumped over the four-foot-wide rockery on the far side of the garden; and then, surprisingly, Ralph followed – just as deftly! It was as though there was not eleven years' age difference between them.

My heart melted – there really was still a lot of life in our old dog!

The following day, just when I thought Ralph couldn't surprise me anymore, after Mads agilely leapt over the stream, Ralph once again followed him, not by using the stone bridge we had put over it, but as Mads had done, over the water itself. I couldn't quite believe his sudden displays of athleticism! He was so old and quite a big dog – he should have been slowing down. Indeed, before Mads' arrival, he had been slowing down; and yet there he was demonstrating this new lease of life.

It's well known among dog circles that if you have a dog who is starting to show their age a little, bringing another younger dog onto the scene can revitalize them – you just have to be careful to make sure their personalities match. It would be awful to bring another dog along and for the older dog to be frightened of them, or, worse, they would end up fighting.

He has all manner of benign lumps and bumps, our Ralphie, which because of his age the vets have recommended leaving and just checking every six months. What if he were to live another four years, or so? Was it better to take those lumps off sooner, while he was that lively, springy boy, rather than waiting and seeing if the lumps would see him through to the end without causing him problems?

Ralph had never been away from us. The thought of him having to be at the veterinary clinic for surgery terrified me, and yet so many dogs endure this when they go for an operation. Brave. I told myself we must all be brave. But it was Ralph: nervous, frightened Ralph. He'd never been brave, so how would we tell him, it was okay? 'You'll be away from us for a day, you'll be sore for a few weeks, but you'll be okay!' But however much I wanted to say that to him, he would not understand. Like so many times, and with so many dogs, I had to remind myself that he was a dog, and I was a human.

But then I, too, had doubts – what if the surgery weakened him? His liver? His kidneys? His heart? He WAS such an old dog! But he wasn't on any pills: there was no arthritis, diabetes, or existing heart problems, and it would all be straightforward surgery – two or three lump removals and perhaps a small dental? His teeth weren't bad, but if there was an opportunity to tidy them up a bit, to see him through, then perhaps we should do that?

Each time I glanced over at him I couldn't help thinking 'Oh Ralphie, what to do?'

Chapter Nineteen

Lumps and Bumps, Dog Hairbrushes, Builders, and The Girl next Door

I took Ralph back to see the vet for a lump-check. We had a long discussion about him and how he was (lively, good appetite, no lameness) and talked about all the ins and outs of him having surgery or not having surgery – and she could see our dilemma. She said she would have the same dilemma if he had been her companion.

People in the veterinary profession sign up to 'do no harm' and giving an anaesthetic to a very old dog to remove a lump which is behaving in a benign way, and which, in the long run may never cause the dog any pain or discomfort if it stays, is an ethical dilemma. We didn't have a crystal ball, we didn't know how long he had left, and weighing the two situations up for his future bothered me, however her comforting words that the lump clearly wasn't bothering him were incredibly valuable.

And so, we came up with a plan. We measured the lumps so we had a baseline and come the following August when he would be due for a booster, we would officially measure them again (although we had to keep measuring them at home to make sure they didn't suddenly grow exponentially). The decision about whether to operate could then be made a bit more objectively and would also be based on blood tests at the time to make sure his kidneys and liver were doing okay.

And so, for then anyway, he had a surgical-reprieve and I decided to stop worrying about him so much and obsessing about the lumps each time I looked at him. I think my problem was related to me being a veterinary nurse, and when I looked at him, or any other dog, I would immediately see the anomalies and abnormalities. That essentially harmless lump was ever-visible to me, meanwhile Alun, Connor and the vet were all happy that he was okay – and we all agreed it was better not to operate.

He had one lump on his rib cage – a lipoma (fatty lump) and another one in his right axillary (armpit) region, which was probably another lipoma but much smaller; those were the two I was most concerned about in case they grew enough to inhibit his movement. He also had a raised, reddish wart-like lump on his left foreleg. There were other similar warty-like lumps, but those were the three we would have been most likely to have done something about – but it would be a lot for an old hound-dog to contend with.

Meanwhile, Mads' grooming sessions continued to come along nicely. He'd also developed a penchant for stealing hairbrushes. At first, he seemed to be playing, so I'd playfully chase him to get the brush back from him (I know, I know, call him back and give him a treat for coming back to me, or do an exchange: 'that's mine, you have this'). I noticed he would get as far as the kitchen and fling the hairbrush back to me. He'd then quickly go and hide or retreat to one of the dog beds. Was he frightened he would be punished for having stolen the hairbrush? These subtleties are things we might miss when we're interacting with our dogs. Instead, I started to do the exchange game with him, despite this, the handles of most of the grooming brushes are quite chewed.

I noticed that he did the same with Nell if she wanted a toy (or a hairbrush!) he had in his mouth; in the middle of getting her to chase him, knowing that was what she wanted, he would fling it back at her. I thought it was strange, because while what he was doing felt like play, it could also have been a survival tactic, i.e.: I have this, you want it, you might hurt me if I don't give it to you, so I'll throw it back to you? This way of being almost submissive, I think, did seem to be helping in his relationship with Nell – to the extent that she was copying his behaviour and sometimes flinging toys (and, yes, hairbrushes too) back to him once she'd finished chewing them or playing with them. I wished I could get inside their heads and understand a little more of how they were interpreting their own actions – were they, perhaps, simply instinctive actions designed to keep the peace?

While all our canine shenanigans were going on,

the builders were ever present, working away at creating our extension and upstairs dormer and Velux windows. Nell and Mads were fascinated by them and would stand and watch them through the back door. What goes through a dog's mind at such times? Do they wonder what on earth is going on, or do they just simply accept that that is the way things are? Did they miss the builders when they had finished? Or did they simply not give them another thought, as building turned to plastering, decorating, and furnishing? Just new days, and humans doing the curious things that humans do.

While the builders had invaded the back of the house, we were busy outside, and we finally got around to replacing the outside perimeter fence which had been temporarily fixed the day after the big storm – the day after Mads had arrived. It took us about three days to complete the task, but at last there was a nice, properly-secure fence on that side of the garden – and one which we were confident would be standing for many years to come. We no longer had to go around and do a fence check before each time we took them into the BG.

The new fence, however, was slatted, whereas the previous one had had no gaps (hence why the wind was able to catch it and push it over). Those nice new gaps which would allow the whistling winds to pass through, however, also allowed the dogs to see the new girl next door.

Next door had never had a dog, but one day a young pup named Baillie had appeared. The dogs had known she was there but had never seen her because of the previously solid fence and her not at that point having been ready to go out into the world. By the time the new fence was up, there she was, a few months old and standing there all pretty, with her black curly hair framing a cute poodle-like face. Mads was beside himself with joy; Nell was initially aloof and disinterested; Ralph took a while to notice her, and one day seemed to finally sense her on the other side of the fence. He happily trotted over to her while wagging his long tail. It looked as though he was saying to her, 'Well, hello little friend, and who might you be?' Meanwhile little Baillie snuffled away at the other side, desperate to reach the face of this large, gentle hound who had oversized ears.

In those days, it was sometimes difficult to know how to get Mads to relax. There were still times when he'd been walked, fed, been out to the garden six times to play or go to the toilet, had a chew at his toys, said hello to Baillie through the fence, been brushed, and still wouldn't settle. His hyperactivity would often go on from after breakfast through to lunchtime. He would whine, hassle the other two and would then have his lunch and go out in the garden as soon as possible after that to play. Eventually, often at about 2pm, we'd heave huge, massive sighs as there was peace at last and we could work.

We realized that on days like those when he wouldn't rest, even though he'd been walked, we had to take him out for a proper good run around for about an hour after breakfast, and it helped.

The situation with Mads reminded me of the great story by Mark Rowlands of his life with a wolf (the Philosopher and the Wolf) and how, to keep the wolf mentally and physically satisfied, he had to take up running with him.

Amid all the commotion, however, we were grateful there were some canine problems we didn't have. Once in a home, food can become a resource over which a group of dogs can become possessive. While this is a problem witnessed in dogs with all sorts of histories (not only rescues), through the years it's something we've seen only once in one of our adopted dogs and that was Oskar the brindle lurcher - Ralph's predecessor. Even with him, however, it lessened when he eventually seemed to realize he didn't need to compete for food... it was coming at regular intervals. He did, though, remain resource-possessive about other things – most memorably the time when he and Dillon were playing with a plastic bottle, only Dillon won the tug of war, at which Oskar grabbed hold of Dillon's whole head. Luckily, we were there to intervene, and everyone came out of the incident unscathed, but we were even more careful after that and could only have playtime with toys with them individually.

These three, Team Ralph, Nell and Mads, willingly allow each other to be around while they're eating, to the extent that they often swap bowls. It is such a nice thing to see, especially when I think of all the people I've known whose dogs have been bothered with food possession – some to the extent that the dog(s) wouldn't even allow the people of the household to touch the bowl when they were eating.

While I'm mentioning food, there is one food-trick I'm sure all canine guardians pull on their dogs when it looks as though Fido is getting a little plump, and that's when the dogs with the biggest belly receive the smallest treats. They don't know... surely? It's quantity (not size) of treats that matters, and the thought that counts?

After months and months of cold and rain, we had a day which was one of those days you wished you could parcel up and open to experience again on those dark, dreary days of winter. Even just to hear the birds chirruping happily in the trees, feel the breeze in our hair, and the warm springtime sun on our faces.

That warm, late spring day, I took the opportunity to split and replant existing herbs and added some new ones; all while the dogs were happily pottering around. We planted dog roses (Rosa canina – what a perfect combination of words) at the front of the house away from the actual canines. Dog roses tend to have horrible thorns, so, strangely, are not the best plants to have around our furry canids. I also put up an extra bird feeder. They're all such simple things, but those are often the best days. I was looking forward to the scent of those gorgeous flowers, I'm not generally a fan of roses, but there is something special about a dog rose. Mum filled our growing up gardens with roses, but even that hasn't made me want to grow them. I think it's the pruning and de-heading – I am a bit of a lazy gardener and like plants to pretty much take care of themselves. It gives me more time to be with the dogs... and to write.

Afterwards, as I settled back in an armchair with the French windows open because it was still warm outside, the heady, refreshing scents of rosemary, thyme, and mint were on my clothes and in my hair, and it felt as though I'd basked in the heart of nature.

I wasn't the only one who had appreciated the day. All three dogs had been enthusiastic to at last be properly outside with us doing things – we had all enjoyed it together (rather than we mere humans standing there shivering as we threw balls for them). Once the playing was over, they were happy to amble about while we dabbled in improving our horticultural skills. The outdoor dog beds made their first appearance of the year, and Ralph and Nell lay and sunbathed. Mads, I don't think, then understood the concept of sunbathing, and spent the whole time out there – four hours – searching for rodents among the rocks of the drystone wall. When he wasn't doing that, he was poking his nose into any hole he found in the ground – just in case there was a rat or mouse poking their nose right back out at him! Thankfully, his nose remained intact!

Four solid hours! And then, they all slept! We hoped for many more days just like that one.

Chapter Twenty

Rodents Again

Mads caught a rat. I suppose it was inevitable with his astute and intense observation of them that he would eventually catch one. We tried to get to him before he pounced, but right from the start, his reactions were too quick for us. Once the poor thing had drawn its last little breath, we put it over in the field where the buzzards or red kites would find it. At least we could do that with any that had not been poisoned.

Later that evening, poor old Ralphie appeared to have hurt his leg – he must have twisted it when he was racing around the garden with Mads, imagining he was ten years younger than he was. As he was still dotting his leg down, I was sure his leg wasn't broken or anything serious. We decided to see how he was the following day and if he was still sore, take him to the vet.

The following morning, he was still sore, and after a poke and a prod, the vet thought it was probably a soft tissue injury and gave him an analgesic. He was sent home on strict rest for two weeks!

Anyone with a dog who loves to go for a walk will know that what the vet requests, and what the dog thinks is going to happen, can be two different things. And so, while he was lying resting, we managed to hide the fact that we were taking the other two out, and one of us stayed with him. And after a week, he was keen to go... so we relented, only sometimes dogs don't know best and vets do, and I suppose I should have overruled him. And so, as limping resumed, we put him on lead exercise in the garden only until he was properly better.

While Ralph used to be terrified of going to see the vet, over time and with much coaxing and kindness, he decided vets and nurses weren't so bad after all – and they liked him too. Knowing how some patients can become quite fractious, I can see how Ralph's gentle nature is appealing. Often dogs are stressed when they're there because the vet might be doing things to them that they don't approve of, there's the smells, the mix of animals, and also because they're there, it usually means there's something up with them in the first place. Apart from his nervousness, Ralph is probably the perfect patient, and the perfect dog. Sometimes in the early days we would say to Nell and Mads, 'Please be more like Ralph,' as we shook our heads in frustration at the two of them.

Years ago, shortly after starting work in the first veterinary practice I worked in, we had a patient named Freddie who was a lurcher, not dissimilar to Ralph. He was such a gentle boy, and one day he came in having cut his front leg. It was the afternoon and he'd had a large feed a few hours earlier, so we couldn't administer a general anaesthetic to him. Instead, he was given a mild sedative and then a local anaesthetic around the wound, and while his humans held on to him, the vet stitched the wound. Even when the local anaesthetic was injected, he didn't flinch. And then, about fifteen minutes later, Freddie was on the floor again, bandaged up, and ready to go home, his tail wagging away as though nothing had happened.

There are very few dogs who would be happy to do that. I feel, though, that Ralph may be one of them. Definitely not Mads, and I'm doubtful, even with all her bandage changes, whether Nell would tolerate it. It's something I saw very rarely in veterinary practice, because, of course, you can't tell a non-human patient what is going on, as even the nicest patients could object. Ethically, as I mentioned before, vets have to be careful to do no harm.

In the early months of Mads, there were some days when cold coffee and cold tea seemed to be the order of the day; they were days when I couldn't remember the last time I'd made myself a hot beverage in daytime and had actually got to drink it in any state except lukewarm or cold.

Why?

Well, more dog politics.

My goodness, they ran me ragged. They were running all of us ragged, actually. I would think back to all the combinations of dogs we'd lived with in the past and, while things had not always been easy, the Fluke/Chip/Jack combination and the Ralph/Peggy/Lucy combinations were, by far, the best and easiest, despite our initial worries about how Peggy would react to little Lucy.

The worst until Nell and Mads' arrival, was the Jack/Dillon (Fluke before him)/Oskar combination, because of Oskar's resource guarding, and most things appearing to have been a resource in his mind. Even with them, though, we quickly found a solution and that solution was splitting Oskar off from the other two whenever we were not in the house. Whenever we were out, he had the luxury of our bedroom, while the other two had the whole of downstairs. It was never ideal, but Oskar arrived with many problems and had been through several homes. It was our way of managing the situation when it became clear he was not always happy with other dogs. It really was the best we could do with a bad situation. At nighttime, Oskar was happy for Jack to join us in what he could easily have seen as his domain. Meanwhile, Dillon, being Connor's dog, simply retired each evening to sleep on his bed with him.

There are times with dogs and their intricate politics, when you simply have to admit that all you can do is manage a situation to make the best that you can out of it for all concerned. Lynn, a wonderful behaviourist I used to know, who is now sadly deceased, used to say that with some dogs you have to do that, just admit that you've tried all you can and that they will never be the perfect dog. Like humans, dogs are rarely perfect – and with some you simply have to find a way to manage the situation whereby the dog is happy and safe. The example she always gave was people who must walk their dog in the very early and late hours to avoid seeing other dogs. It's not the best solution, but when all other ways (humane, of course) have been tried and the dog is fearful or stressed by other dogs, then why not do that for them? It's a small price to pay to have a contented dog, for who knows for sure what goes on inside their minds and what fears they might have when they're in contact with other dogs. With walks at a safer time of day, the dog can spend the rest of their time peacefully pottering around the house and garden.

And so, we arrived at a situation with our Ralph/Nell/Mads combination whereby Nell and Mads couldn't both be off lead at the same time in the BG. They just couldn't. I'd tried all the tricks in the book, and they became wise to any tricks we had available to us. We had had that peace, but then when Baillie arrived and she was outside in her garden, they would become like wild creatures leaping at the fence. Initially, they both had to remain on leads until she went in, or else Nell would snap at her through the gaps in the fence, and Mads wouldn't leave her alone, even learning from Nell that snapping through the fence was fun. If they couldn't reach her (which they couldn't because the fence slats were too close to one another), they sometimes redirected their frustration towards each other. Or they sometimes redirected at Ralph, as Ralph himself had become prone to having the odd bark at Baillie. It had become chaotic.

We set about rewarding them by scattering food whenever they didn't go near the fence, so essentially the fence, and next door's dog, became something much less of a distraction. This was unless, of course, they were having positive communications with the little curly-topped, raven-haired pooch – which they occasionally did, and then they would be rewarded for that. Ralph would often just sniff her and have a little friendly woof, so he was not a problem, but we couldn't teach the other two at the same time as each other... and so, opportunistic training of one dog at a time had to be the norm – for a while anyway, until they realized that little Baillie wasn't going anywhere. She had become like the fourth dog in their sometimes-dysfunctional group. As she got bigger, she was sometimes partial to having a little go at them through the fence. We felt awful that our three scoundrels (two really) may have taught her to behave that way.

Chapter Twenty-One
Where Were You Before?

One windy, rainy afternoon after braving the elements to take the dogs out for a mooch about, I watched one of the dog rescue programmes on TV – essential watching for the dogs as they were all settled down beside me, of course. Two dogs were rescued from a house where they had been neglected to the point that one was so emaciated, she had to be euthanized. The people the dogs lived with got away with such abject cruelty because they disappeared from the grid. Vanish! Never brought to justice.

The circumstances are different in Ralph and Mads' cases, in that although they were both skinny when rescued, they were not emaciated. However, there is similarity between both the case on the TV and Mads' and Ralph's cases, in that they had all clearly suffered and were abandoned to fend for themselves. And the people who did that to them have all got away with it – just like the people who previously lived with all strays and animals they abandoned.

I've often wondered through all these years with Ralph whether the people who were cruel to him had other dogs at the time or whether they went on to have other dogs. The thought that this could be (is probably) the case, horrifies me. In the early years, I used to dread someone coming along and saying he was their dog. Now Ralph is old, and that time of worrying about someone saying he was theirs has long since passed. The thought persists, though, that whoever those people were, they are still out there, oblivious to his rescue. I suppose I can only hope that somehow, in some other way, those people have been brought to justice and have had their comeuppance for such neglect or possible cruelty.

These days, as I watch the three dogs resting and contented, I feel so angry with those people who stole the years of their lives before they came to live with us. They must be either detached and uncaring, in Mads' and Ralph's cases, turning them onto the streets or allowing them to stray. In Nell's case, racing dogs until they no longer make money for them. How many other dogs have those people hurt to the point that the dog emotionally closes down and gives up – their first reaction in a situation becoming fear? How many of those dogs are left behind, not managing to escape their dire situation?

On arrival with us, Mads was without doubt the worst behaved dog we had ever known. Even as people who 'know about dogs' he was a massive challenge to us. And what of the people who had him before – do they have any other animals? I desperately hope not. His problems were preventable if he had received the proper care when he was a puppy and younger dog.

Is this a key problem with strays, in that dogs are rescued from the streets, and unless those people are known and prosecuted and banned from keeping animals, it's possible they will go on to replace them? Prosecutions these days rarely result in a lifelong ban from keeping animals, or even a lifelong ban on keeping a specific species, so after a ten-year ban, for instance, someone can quite easily and legally get themselves another dog. If, for instance, the person who previously had Ralph had been prosecuted all those years ago, the likelihood would be that they could now legally be in charge of another dog. And that thought is terrifying – I shall never understand why lifelong bans have become so rare.

Nell's racing handler at least handed her to a rescue, many thousands of greyhounds suffer a much worse fate. But is it ethical to race greyhounds? Greyhounds deserve so much more than the unpredictable lifestyle they're given, and so much more than being cast aside at four years old or less; so much more than a life in which skeletal and muscular injuries are the norm. What would I say to her handler if ever I met them? I would ask them how they could not see that this beautiful girl is worth more than a life of racing and all that that entails. I would say, 'Why do you do this? Why do you disregard the needs of greyhounds? Why is money worth more than their health and their lives? Why can't you see the emotional damage you have done to this beautiful, graceful dog?'

Through the many years we have lived with Ralph, in my head I have rehearsed many times what I would say to the person who hurt him and then dumped him on the streets. How, in a country such as the UK, can someone get away with this? If confronted with them, my first question would not be about Ralph, it would be: 'How many more were there?'

And I truly don't think I would want to wait around to hear their response. Because what if when we first brought Ralph home, we had had had some means of finding that person? Would any good have come of it? How can you prove cruelty when the dog is no longer with that person and there are no witnesses to the acts of cruelty.

And Mads. What on earth happened to make him the way he was when he arrived with us? He was absolutely terrified of being stroked, he wouldn't make eye contact, he didn't want anyone to be behind him or to restrain him for brushing or to check his eyes, ears, or teeth. He was the most broken dog we'd ever lived with.

Beyond their reactions when they arrived and the assumptions we have made about what happened to them before, with Ralph and Mads, there is that feeling that there must have been other people who were around them who have turned the other cheek. There must be those who were family and friends who knew what was going on and who are therefore complicit in the cruelty. I know I don't know for sure what happened with either dog, but dogs have cavernous emotional depths, and they remember – and both dogs' persisting fears absolutely must have been a result of what happened to them before.

Chapter Twenty-Two
That Recall Problem

One of the most important things we should teach our dogs is to come back when called. Getting a dog to return to you or 'wait' are probably the most important messages we want them to respond to. Sit, though, does it really matter whether a dog can sit on command? Not at all, just as long as you can get them to remain in one place when you need them to. And therein lay the problem!

For a long time, Mads had the most awful recall. His progress was initially hindered by his lack of desire to approach us, to focus on us, or even allow us to be present in the little mixed-up mess of a world in which he'd found himself. But then, at last, having done some work with him in the house on 'wait' and getting him to lie down or sit, we made a little progress. He seemed to like doing that, even though he thought 'sit' meant lie down, and also that lie down meant lie down; but it didn't really matter if he plonked his whole self on the ground whenever we mentioned sit when trying to communicate with him. We were desperately trying to find out what he knew and what he had no clue about.

And so, we practised this, and each time he got it right in his little Madsy way, he received a treat. We applied the same approach outside when he was off lead. He would wait, I'd approach him and give him a treat and sometimes I'd get him to do a 'sit' (and, of course, he'd lie down), but then I'd let him go on his way to play some more so he wouldn't see the reward as a trick to capture him. Progress was slow, though, as he was easily distracted, particularly by Baillie next door. In the early months, when she was out in her garden, no amount of squeaking of toys or offers of treats would suffice, until she had lost interest in him.

In the end, we resorted to a double panel fence arrangement, whereby we doubled up the panels on the bottom half of the new fence so we could give our dogs a sense of separation from her, and vice versa. They were still able to see and hear one another, but the reactions gradually became much less intense, enabling us and our neighbour to work with our dogs with fewer distractions.

With the doubling up of the panels, they were not close enough to snap at each other through the gaps, hence the 'fun' was taken out of the situation. For the most part, it helped, and we could all finally work on those finer aspects of deciphering our dogs' emotional intricacies. After all, our dogs' interactions with Baillie were holding her back at that time too, as they were just as much of a distraction to her.

What is it that makes a dog so terrified to come back when they are outside and you're desperately wanting or needing them to return to you? It's true that some of this is undoubtedly embedded in the fact that distractions are often far more exciting than going back on your lead and into the house or car, but with Mads it appeared to be much more deep-rooted than that.

Again, I was making assumptions, but he could have been punished in the past for having a poor recall. Alun thought it was possible he'd been hit with a lead, and it was actually the lead he was frightened of. For that reason, we diligently hid the lead in a pocket and only attached it to him once he appeared to be feeling comfortable enough to be reattached. We were constantly having to take the tiniest steps with him to ensure he didn't go into emotional overload and take several steps back. Essentially, we were guessing, and desperately trying to find ways of working with him that wouldn't induce fear reactions.

People who punish their dog when they eventually return to them make me so angry. What motivation does the poor dog ever have to return? And then such dogs are rehomed (or turned onto the streets) for their apparent disobedience, and the fearful behaviour is passed onto other people who, with all the love in the world for the dog, spend months (years sometimes) in breaking down those negative emotions.

When I lived in the city, I would sometimes see people in the parks punishing their dogs for not having an immediate recall. Why did they have their dog off a lead without a reliable recall? If ever I was close enough, I would call over and tell them not to hit their dog, and add that the non-return was their fault, not the dog's. I've had verbal abuse screamed at me and arms waved angrily, a chain lead thrust in the air at me (the one the woman was using to hit the dog); meanwhile, strangers in the park who also witnessed what had happened, just walked on by.

Some years ago, in a forest where we were walking, there was a couple out with a few dogs. The man called all three to come back to him, and just two of them came back straight away. Once he arrived back, the other one got hit across the face for his slow return. I was so, so angry but not brave enough to say anything on that occasion, for fear of being hit myself. And I so regret not having told him what a despicable person he was, and that the dog's reluctant recall was all his fault. The dog came back – the man should have been rewarding the dog for returning, however long it took. The words 'Good boy' in a happy voice can do so much to help dogs learn and want to return to you.

Perhaps with phone videos now, if someone is quick enough then the person can quickly be filmed, and the film sent to the RSPCA or the police. But how do you find where the person lives? That was my problem with the chain-yielding woman – I had no idea where she lived and no evidence of what she had done to her dog – and no one else around appeared to care.

Returning to what I was talking about in terms of the poor treatment it seems Ralph and Mads experienced in their former lives, those who may have observed such acts were complicit in what happened, the same goes for the person with the man with the three dogs. But perhaps she was frightened of him too? I only hope that if that was the case and she felt unable to protect herself and the dogs, that she's managed to rescue herself and the dogs from that situation.

Chapter Twenty-Three

Dogs – When the End Arrives

As human companions to our animals, we have a duty of care to ensure they don't suffer – but as the end of their life draws near and we begin to see a level of suffering, we are handed a decision we perhaps want to avoid. We hope with all our hearts when they become infirm and their lives are nearly over, that they will just drift off to sleep one night and not wake up. For most dogs, though, that decision of life and death is in the hands of the people in their lives – dogs have no choice in when, where, or how. And this is where the choice you make, whether guided by the vet, or as a decision you've made independently, can become one of the worst and most difficult decisions you can ever make – and one which will live with you forevermore.

I've seen both ends of the scale – those who couldn't care less, and those for whom the loss of their animal is one of the most tragic breaking of bonds they will ever encounter. How do we make that decision? Palliative care is a tool used far less in animals than it is in humans – and it is probably because with animals we have the capacity to legally end their life. But is it always right? I struggle with this because as a vegan all life is precious, and yet when you see an animal you love wasting away as they no longer want to eat, they've become incontinent, they are gasping for air, in pain because of old injuries or aged joints and the painkillers are no longer working, you know you have that option. You know that you can end their suffering – and so, for most of us, we do.

The problem is that if they could choose, would they choose to end their life there? Then? In that way? We have no way of knowing, for they have no concept of the means that we have to make that decision on their behalf, and thus we make the decision for them and ask the vet to go in with the needle. And then, it's over. All we're left with as humans is the massive sense of loss, and the awful feeling in your gut about whether or not you did the right thing. Did we do it for them? Or did we do it for ourselves to ease the suffering we felt at seeing them suffering? It's such a tricky thing and I've seen animals experience prolonged suffering while their humans kick about that decision which will change everything. Conversely, animals who quite clearly were not ready to go.

Dogs seem to know that something is up. When we knew our little terrier Lucy's time was getting near, we grappled with the decision. She was ill, wasting away, blind, deaf, struggling to walk, falling over, bumping into things, and sleeping the deepest (yet not peaceful) sleeps. She wasn't far from the end, and on the two nights before we finally asked the vet to euthanize her, Ralph spent those evenings with his body curled around hers. Holding her, comforting her, and we were sure he knew she didn't have long left.

It was a very emotional time, seeing him doing that, because while his bond had been strong with Peggy, he'd always been a little wary of this little dog Lucy with the tiny, occasionally snarling mouth. But in those hours, he was there for her. It was such a sad thing, and yet in a way it was beautiful, that somehow, he knew that something was wrong with her. He overcame all his nervousness and found something inside him which would allow him to comfort his little adversary. In those precious hours, Lucy would sometimes become aware of his presence and would nestle down into the warmth of this big, soft-hearted dog.

In making that decision to have a dog euthanized, some say it can be useful to write down all the things they used to love doing and see whether they are still able to do those things. If they're old and infirm, however, some of those things will have fallen away naturally anyway and have been replaced by other gentler activities. It would be unfair to suggest, then, that because the dog can no longer enjoy a five mile hike each morning that their quality of life is poor, especially if they are still managing to have a nice little snuffle around the garden whenever they go out to the toilet. I think people will know whether their dog's quality of life is poor – and these are probably for all of the reasons I listed previously for Lucy. There will be a deep gut feeling that it might be possible to rid the dog of that suffering. Someone once described it to me as being that one last kindness, but I have difficulty believing that, and think now that we tend to simply do our best with a very bad situation. Having been a part of so many people's grief at losing their animals, I feel confident that almost all of those cases were for the right reasons.

Ralph wasn't doing great. We were still not sure of the exact location of his pain, but it was slowly getting better. Beyond that, he'd been getting us up several times in the night and I suspected there was something going on with his urinary tract. One lunch time I got a urine sample from him. As a veterinary nurse, you get to know what normal urine looks like and if there's something quite wrong, it is sometimes obvious (too dilute, too concentrated, blood etc.,). What emerged into the pot from Ralph was clearly not 'normal' urine. It was reddish and looked very concentrated. I immediately took the sample into the house and stuck one of my urine dipsticks in it: right enough, there was blood, but also protein. Protein in urine can be a sign of kidney failure, but protein in concentrated urine, as this was (rather than dilute and particularly in a dog who is otherwise fit and well), is often a sign of a urinary tract infection (UTI).

And so, off I headed with him to the veterinary surgery for a proper diagnosis, and yes, it was probably a UTI but they took a blood sample as well, and Ralph and I headed home with a course of antibiotics for him. Later that day I received a phone call from the vet to say his blood sample was clear and his liver and kidneys were functioning normally – I can't express how happy that made me feel. I knew with every bone in my body that Ralph was getting old, I could see that every day; I knew he was. He was so very precious to me, to us all. And it's incredibly difficult when you see someone you love fading.

The infection didn't pass quite as easily as we hoped. His urine was sent away to check for bacterial sensitivity to antibiotics and we knew the antibiotic he was on was the right one. In the end, because the infection was so stubborn, it took almost six weeks of antibiotics before the infection was gone and our dear Ralph was rejuvenated! While he was still not one hundred percent (antibiotics can take a lot out of you, especially if you've taken them for a while), one lunchtime when I opened the gate to the BG, he went charging in as though he'd found his puppyhood again.

I truly hoped that all that had been going on with him had simply been a blip. I was so relieved that he was finally off the tablets! He'd got to the stage that whenever I approached him with his pills, he clamped his jaws together and if I got his mouth open, he'd somehow developed a way of fixing his tongue to the roof of his mouth – it was bizarre and not like anything I'd seen in other dogs.

The tablets he was on were luckily crushable tablets, and so, like generations of humans have done, I resigned myself to the crushing and putting in some water method, drawing it into a syringe and squirting it behind his canine teeth. He was still not impressed, but it beat forcing his mouth open. What was interesting was that the tablets were labelled as being palatable, but just like the worm tablet labels which suggest the same thing, they're anything but. You hand the tablet to the dog like a treat, and they look at you and back to the tablet, and then back at you again, clearly horrified that you would even think they would believe that such a thing was a treat. Don't ever believe a label that has the words 'palatable tablets' written on it – it's a blatant lie! Dogs know!

As Ralph recovered from all his medical traumas, summer flowers were in full bloom and filled the garden with shades of white, pink, yellow, orange, and purple. The warmer months can fill you with optimism and hope, and the days were long. At dusk each night, we'd all go and wait in the garden for the pipistrelle bats to come and swoop, duck, and dive over our heads as we leaned back in the garden chairs and watched them. All three dogs lay beside us – not really understanding what the strange flying creatures were.

But then, as if we hadn't had plenty of days

visiting the vet, Mads developed a bad limp. It was a hot, sunny day and while Nell and Ralph basked in the Scottish sunshine, Mads continued to run around as though he wasn't covered in thick, fluffy fur and the stream which he would often go into to have a drink and cool off, hadn't dried up. And then, somehow, he twisted himself as he came down to land after taking a huge leap into the air to catch the ball.

Off to the vets we went, and just like with Ralph, she was pretty sure it was soft tissue damage, so he was given a week of painkillers and put on strict rest! Ah, that strict rest again! But he really was sore, and the pain must have been breaking through the analgesics a little, so he was quieter than usual. After a week, he was still limping quite badly, so we booked him in for the following day for another examination by the vet. If nothing obvious could be found in the clinic, he was to stay in for some x-rays.

The next day arrived, and on examination of him and palpation of his leg, there was nothing obvious wrong, we therefore had to leave him with them until mid-afternoon. We missed him so much – even Nell was mellowing and gave him a happy greeting when he returned. Luckily, there were no bone or joint problems, and he was given a longer course of painkillers. It took several weeks (sometimes these things do) and we gradually increased his exercise, taking a step or two back when he showed any more signs of limping. Eventually, he was well again –

and back to leaping in the air to catch balls and toys.

Ralph, meanwhile, was in his element and joining us on greyhound rescue meetups. Nell had blotted her copybook early on by growling and snapping at a couple of her greyhound friends, so Ralph had become the greyhound representative for the whole household. And he loved it, buddying up with his new, slender, hound-dog friends. I don't think they realized he was an imposter and had never seen a greyhound track in his life.

After one walk we did with him in that September – the annual Great Global Greyhound Walk – we were gathered around chatting and about twenty greyhounds (and Ralph) were still there. Ralph suddenly became interested in something lurking beside a bush about ten feet away from us. It was a black cat – a very brave or very reckless one! The strange thing was that Ralph was the only dog who noticed the cat, and as we walked to the car about ten minutes later, the cat followed us, swishing his tail as he marched along. Still, none of the other hounds noticed him, just Ralph, who was mesmerized by his new feline friend.

Once Mads was on the mend, he resumed his love of DIY. He was always in on the action. When the builders had finished the extension's external walls, and we had to sort out the interior by framing up, putting up plasterboard, plastering, fitting the fire and so on, there was a huge pile of plasterboard in the middle of the room. While Ralph and Nell would politely walk around the pile of boards, Mads used the plasterboard as a springboard to get from one part of the extension to another. In the end, we kept one sacrificial piece on the top of the pile, a piece which could get scratched and covered in pawprints. A few others made their way onto the walls with his pawprints on them. We felt quite sad plastering and painting over them. It was as though his signature was creatively plastered (pun intended) all over the house!

Garden time became special time when the dogs could wander about snuffling the ground, all eagerly catching the scents of creatures who had passed through on their own life's journey. When the sun broke through the familiar Scottish clouds, they would lie out there on the outdoor dog beds, watching the birds on the feeders or in the trees. Mads would take the occasional punt at catching them, which I was sure he knew he was not allowed to do.

On days when it was cold or rainy, the three of them inhabited the sofas indoors, somehow making the connection that the weather on their morning walk was an indication of what the weather would be like later on in the back garden. Perhaps it was in the way that we humans behaved when the weather was gloomy, and instead of being all enthusiastic to get outdoors and do outdoorsy things, we resigned ourselves to being indoors, our body language telling them, 'Let's just stay inside today.'

I always loved the mornings when they'd had their breakfast and they were waiting for the rest of the day to begin, the times when they would curl up or lie on their backs and kick back and relax. It was at times like those that I watched them and felt such pride with each of them at how far they'd all come. While music played in the background and I sat at my desk writing, the dogs would be suspended in deep, soothing relaxation. Yet I knew there had been times when they'd all had to struggle to survive mentally – through fear, exhaustion, and loneliness; all of that in a world which didn't understand they needed safety and a chance to express their true selves.

I loved to watch Mads as he was sprawled across the beanbag, which he had finally managed to negotiate his way around, and which was surrounded by an array of cushions; his eyes would be tightly closed and his breathing steady. Ralph and Nell were often like bookends on the sofa, again with tightly closed eyes and their chests rising and falling – almost in synchronicity with one another. At times like those it appeared that none of them had a care in the world.

Chapter Twenty-Four

Gotcha Day

It's a modern conception, the social media influenced Gotcha Day, and one which is marked with all manner of treats, toys, and doggie birthday cake. There is no doubt it must be lucrative for canine apparel and dog treat businesses. I must make a huge admission of guilt here, however, that we had never celebrated the gotcha day of any of our rescue dogs until that first 'gotcha' day with Mads.

So, why Mads? What made him so special? Why should he have been the first? I've thought about this a lot, and I think it's because he came so far in the change from the dog who arrived a year earlier, to the dog he became twelve months later. But Ralph, too, changed hugely! It took years for him to finally feel comfortable and at ease with, well, life, I suppose. With Mads, the change was monumental, and I suppose the Gotcha Day thing was something much more than when Connor jokes that, 'Mads is the favoured child.' I suppose Mads became for us the epitome of what rescue should look like; and on his journey we watched each miniscule, incremental change, and were in awe at each step he made along the way.

But Gotcha Day was never going to just be about Mads. Ralph and Nell would also get their new toys and special treats, because they are all special, they had all had their own journeys to that point – a rocky road at times, but they all triumphed!

There are a couple of local words from places I've lived that I used a lot during that first year whenever I talked about Mads. In the early nineties, I lived in Cumbria for three years. A friend I met there used the word 'ratching' a lot: 'having a ratch about,' 'had a good ratch for it.' It basically means to search for something and Mads did an awful lot of that 'ratching' about. He was usually searching for those all-important, unsuspecting creatures to chase. It wasn't until one day when I was talking about Mads' antics and I mentioned he'd been 'ratching about,' that my brother said, 'That's a good Cumbrian word,' that I realized it had been part of my own vocabulary for the few decades since I'd left Cumbria. It made me think of those times when I'd used the word when I was teaching, most of my students must have wondered what on earth I was talking about when I'd lost something (which happened a lot), and I told them I'd had a good ratch for whatever it was.

The other word I used a lot about Mads during that time was one I picked up here in Scotland! 'Clipe,' meaning to tell on someone… and as Mads' character developed, he revealed himself to be such a clipe! Each morning when Alun was up working in the hills with the wind turbines, Connor had gone to work in his office, and I was still getting the day started but doing lots of things like giving the dogs their breakfast, loading the dishwasher, and generally tidying up before starting work, I realized Mads had a strict time schedule. And woe betided me if I was late feeding them or giving them a treat. If that happened and I didn't immediately do something when he 'asked' in his own inimitable way, then he would go marching off to find Connor. Once there, he'd 'tell' Connor of his current predicament with a loud, demanding bark! And then the two of them would quickly come back to me to see what it was that Mads was looking for. Proud Mads would slink along behind Connor, swaying his Basil Brush tail and looking ever so sleekit (another local word, but Scottish this time, which means sly). Each time he did this, the 'problem' was usually something like the dog bowls were still soaking and I hadn't yet fed them their second breakfast (they're like hobbits in that way).

Strangely, If I had done everything he expected at the regular time, then he wouldn't do it. One time, he even looked up at the sink and sniffed the air and then gave me one of his sidelong glances... was he actually checking to see whether I'd put the bowls in to soak? We'd never had a dog in our lives who was quite as clever as Mads... and perhaps that was a factor in the relative speed of his healing!

As a species, we humans have no other species in the world that understands us quite like dogs do. It fascinates me every day how much they understand about us and our language – verbal and non-verbal. Non-verbally, they notice subtle changes in our expressions and movements, and these let them know how we're feeling. Are we happy, sad, angry, fearful, disgusted? Our faces tell them pretty much all they need to know.

Verbally, they interpret tone and volume, knowing that the louder we get when calling them, the more urgent it is that they return. With words, though, I'm amazed at how they pick up on words in sentences and put these together with our hand movements and tone/volume of voice and do what you need them to do at that time. Whole sentences seem to pose no great barrier to our communication:

'Go and find Ralph (or Nell, or Connor, or Dad, or Mum),' And off he goes.

'Do you want to go to the garden?'

'Would you like a peanut butter sandwich.' (All three dogs' special treat).

'It's dinner time.'

'It's time for bed.'

'It's time to go for a walk.'

'Let's go and feed the birds!'

'Time to go in.'

And so on.

And sure, they are probably just picking up on the key words, but it's amazing that any other species can do this so naturally and seemingly effortlessly. There's one phrase I'm not sure they really get though, and that's, 'in a minute.' Do they understand that it's not just now, but soon, that whatever they are hoping will happen will actually happen? I don't know.

They also learn words and sounds which lead them to acquiring something they become fond of, for instance, when Mads arrived in our lives he had a terribly dry coat. To remedy this problem, the first vet I worked with used to recommend a small knob of margarine or advise putting a bit of vegetable oil in a dog's food twice a week.

It turned out that Mads was partial to a little sunflower margarine on the end of your finger. Right from the start, he loved it to the degree that he quickly learned where it was kept and how to access it. Once learned, whenever we were making food and we happened to lift the lid off the tub, he would appear beside us in a matter of seconds, his big, brown eyes staring up at the yellow and white container. We don't use margarine that often, so he tends to get his small reward pretty much every time it's used. And, of course, Ralph and Nell must have a tiny margarine curl too.

He was also partial to sunflowers themselves, it seemed. One day when I'd put him on a lead to take him back in the house (before his recall was reliable), as we walked past a sunflower we'd been nurturing, he reached over and pulled the head off it and flung it behind us. I had to laugh at him – he was such a monkey!

While there have been many times, I'm sure, when Ralph and Nell have cursed the day we brought Mads to live with us, as time passed it became obvious that they could see there were benefits too. He became so very in control of the goings-on in the house – at keeping his humans in check, that naturally they benefited too. Mads demonstrated many 'learned' behaviours – behaviours animals learn, usually for survival, rather than those that are genetic. They were behaviours Ralph and Nell didn't need to bother to learn, because he did them for them. When he asked for his morning veggie sausage, for instance (one which doesn't contain onion or garlic, as both are toxic to dogs), they'd all get one. For Ralph and Nell, beyond sharing in his Gotcha Day, there were also clearly food-acquisition advantages to Mads being in ours and thus, their, lives.

Chapter Twenty-Five

And Now

When I see Mads racing around the garden, seemingly without a care in the world, when he throws himself on the hillock we created with the earth from underneath our house extension, and then he happily rolls over and rubs himself in hedgehog poop, those are the times when I understand the essence of what rescue is about. It's taking a dog from the world they knew, one in which they were probably badly treated, perhaps even loathed, and showing them that the world can be all right – they can be free of that fear and horror. Indeed, they can even get to the point whereby they are essentially in charge of their own life and (in Mads' case anyway) the lives of everyone around them. But most of all, it's about showing them what love is. There are some dogs who never know that love, and a fine line sometimes between gaining that place where they will be loved or one in which they will only be seen as a nuisance, or worse.

As I write this, outside there is a hard frost on the ground and the weather people are promising snow in the next few days. While Mads still wants to go out for a run around, walks with the three of them are cut short by getting from A to B as quickly as possible – it is Mads' second winter with us and so very cold out there. Even with him being the little tough nut that he is, however, those runs around outside that he normally insists on having whatever the weather, are cut short, with little resistance from him at having to come inside and having to endure relaxing in the comfort of an armchair. Instead, he lay watching the birds through the window as they were going about their winter survival business.

There is no resistance from Ralph and Nell to not be outdoors running around and playing – it's as though their bodies are superglued to the sofas. I have never known two dogs to sleep so much. Ralph can surely be excused as he's an old dog now, but Nell? Nell is only nearly seven years old!

Greyhounds are often referred to as couch potatoes, and Nell definitely lives up to this – it is her motto for life and one which she lives by with the greatest amount of enthusiasm a dog could possibly muster. When she does run, she is incredibly fast, but, for the most part, she just doesn't bother. She enjoys her walks, though, and will potter along with the other two, sniffing at new scents and looking out for other dogs. She looks for them so she can show me she can restrain herself by not barking at them, and instead get treats for being such a good girl.

The sights, smells, and sounds on a walk are essential to a dog's mental health, and when they come across something they've never experienced, that only adds to their mental and environmental enrichment. Dogs can be surprised by the strangest things, but it's rare for all three to be startled by the same thing...

It was one of those dark, moonless nights when the stars were hidden by clouds. I love windy days, and this was a particularly breezy night. Then, suddenly, there in the distance along the streetlamp lit road, we saw something tumbling about and bouncing up and down on the tarmac. We all became quiet as our fright, flight, fight, fawn instincts told us to be careful. As we tentatively got closer, we realized there was more than one... perhaps six, no, even more than that! These strange things were being blown about by the breeze and appeared to be bouncing along the road.

All three dogs' ears sprang up on top of their heads, Ralph growled (yes, Ralph!), and Nell and Mads jumped around on the end of their leads, not knowing whether to go towards these strangely moving things or to run away – their own fright, fight, flight, fawn instincts also working overtime.

Acknowledgement of novel things in an animal's environment is essential, and beyond that, there's sense in that 'caution equals survival' approach to strange happenings, and even Ralph was actively taking part in the excitement. Initially we didn't know what they were, and even we had a few moments of not knowing whether to run and hide.

But then the humans amongst us realized what those strange bouncing objects were... and felt a little silly. Our neighbours a few doors down the road have the most beautiful hydrangea bushes – one pink, one blue. The pink one is huge and surrounded by a dry-stone wall. Each year, both bushes brighten the street with their massive pink and mauve flowers; in winter the flowers die away, all their giant, domed flowers turning brown. These dead flower heads must be pruned to allow for the next year's giant flowers – and that's exactly what our neighbours must have done earlier that day, for in the wind, all their neatly piled ten-inch diameter (they really are that huge) flower heads were blowing from their garden and heading like tumbleweed down the road.

As it was bouncing along, Connor managed to very quickly grab one of the hydrangea heads and showed it to Ralph, and once he'd sniffed it, that settled him down. I was a bit behind them with Nell and one of them came blowing past me – Nell saw what it was, so that settled her too.

Mads, though, was beside himself, barking and doing convolutions in the air. And then, one came near to him, and he cowered to the ground – he was terrified of it. As quickly as it had come near him, it rolled on back down the road again. Connor took the one he had in his hand over to show Mads. Mads sniffed it and seemed to acknowledge it was okay; it was nothing to fear. Then his alert, collie-like mind seemed to remember the one that had just flown past him on its bouncy journey. His gaze shifted in that direction and then quickly back to Connor. It was just as though he was asking, 'Well, this is all well and good, but what about THAT one?'

Like Mads, Nell has come a very long way since her arrival in our home. She has some quirky, adorable habits and in her quiet, 'sitting back and watching what Mads is up to' way (to also be read as 'watching what Mads might be trying to extract from the humans of the house'), she has learned a lot from him.

It's Nell I tend to walk, while Alun walks Mads, and Connor walks Ralph, and she very quickly learned about the benefits of the treat pouch I attach to my jeans belt loop. The treats serve their purpose as a distraction from cats and other dogs, but Nell knows that even when there are no other dogs around, all she needs to do is nudge the bag and my hand automatically reaches in and gets her a treat. If it's a treat she's not so keen on, she'll take it anyway and keep on nudging until one of her favourite ones emerges from the bag. I sometimes feel I have no other function than that of a giant dog treat dispenser. Recently I've been working on her looking up at me when she sees other dogs, rather than nudging the bag – for fear of her making her big, greyhound nose sore!

She clearly struggled with Mads when he first came along, and of course, there was that awful spate of spontaneous aggression towards us, which was time-limited over a period of about five or six months and then just stopped. Perhaps she had been in pain, or perhaps it was the stress of the house renovations – we still don't know, but she learned to live with us, and we learned to live with her.

She's now even happy for Mads to round her up on his morning 'time for a walk everyone,' tour of the house he insists on doing. If she and Ralph are not yet up (as Mads still sleeps downstairs on the sofa in Connor's bedroom) and I'm still getting dressed or fiddling with my hair, then he comes upstairs to collect us. He marches around like a cat with his tail in the air – moving like a cat, too, rubbing himself along the edge of the bed – and then he goes over to their beds and sniffs them. 'C'mon, lazy bones hounds, it's time to go for a walk,' he seems to be saying to them.

And it works – with Nell anyway, as she eases herself out of her bed. Then the two of them march to the landing and do a side by side stretch together at the top of the stairs – often stretching four or five times in synchronicity before they head down – perhaps delicately re-establishing their group dynamics. Nell proceeds downstairs first, with Mads giving her a chance to make a head start. He then ambles down behind her – not by chasing her (the kind of thing even Ralph would have done in his younger years), but in an incredibly calm, gentle way. It's as though he's her best buddy and is watching out for her. Does he sense that even now she is quite nervous of stairs as she quite gingerly embarks on negotiating each step, I wonder?

Ralph, though, although Mads goes and chivvies him along, and sometimes Ralph follows, more often he tends to wait for me. The bond between Ralph and me is so long-established that a little upstart like Mads is going to have difficulty gaining ground, especially when the alternative for Ralph is to spend a few extra minutes in his bed and wait for me instead.

Ralph used to have what seemed like horrific dreams in the years after he first arrived. As the years passed, they lessened – they still happen from time to time, but they're in no way as violent. A gentle wake up, and despite his now cataracted, opaque eyes and reduced (sometimes selective, I'm sure) hearing, he quickly remembers he's safe, and those monsters of his nightmares can no longer hurt him.

While he is an old man now, Ralph continues to have regular sparks of joyful play when he goes down on his front legs and does a play bow, sometimes adding a playful Ralphie 'woof' as he does so. I don't know how much time we have left with him, and I hope I never have to make the decision to let him go – I think most of us humans long for that. Perhaps with him, one night when his time has come, he will simply drift to sleep beside me and not wake up, easing his way peacefully into whatever lies beyond our world.

Chapter Twenty-Six

And Onwards

Like many people who live with and love dogs, I often wonder about what comes next. I know we all wonder that about ourselves, but our dogs, too, they have a life, they feel emotions, and all that must come from somewhere. When they pass away, what happens then?

At risk of seeming a little off the wall, or even eccentric, perhaps what recently happened with Ralph might offer some clue. We were making breakfast and the other two had followed us into the kitchen. Ralph remained alone in the sitting room, and I began to wonder if he was okay, so I walked back through and stood in the doorway watching him. Without him being aware that I was standing there, I observed the strangest thing.

He was dancing around, going down on his front end, and playing like he would occasionally do with other dogs... but there was no other dog (or even toys) in front of him. He was down low on the carpet and having the best, fun time. I don't know what he could see, but he was playing in the way he used to play with little Lucy. In his mind, I'm sure he was aware of a dog in front of him. My logical mind tells me that perhaps he was simply playing with his own shadow, but it seemed like so much more than that – and although he's getting older, he absolutely has all his faculties.

That's not the first time I've seen such a thing happen. When I was a teenager, we had a dog who used to lie under the television table. He'd watch us as we all gathered around to watch TV. I'm not sure why Prince chose that place – perhaps he felt safe from all the hustle and bustle and felt comforted that he knew where we all were. When the vet advised he be put to sleep because of his repeated epilepsy, we soon found another rescue dog: Beauty.

Beauty settled in really quickly, and lived to be fifteen, but in those early years in that house, she never lay underneath the TV table. She would often be found staring at or interacting with what she could see under there. We were all sure she had some notion of Prince being there (or at least having been there), but the level-headed, objective part of me says that perhaps there was simply a residual scent of him.

But then, it's not only our dogs who appear to have these strange experiences, we humans do too. One morning when we were still living in our last house, I was giving the dogs some morning treats from a treat bag. Once I'd given Ralph and Lucy theirs, I turned to give some to the large black dog who was standing next to me, reaching her head up for a biscuit. I absentmindedly reached down to hand her the treat, but then I realized with the heaviest heart that there was no other dog – Peggy had died a week earlier. This apparition of a dog was standing exactly where Peggy would have been standing to wait for treats. To me, on that morning, I have no doubt that I saw Peggy standing right next to me. The experience took my breath away and I had to sit down to try to figure out what I'd seen. I'm not religious, I don't know what makes these things happen, but it made me seriously believe that there must be something else, and that whatever that something is, our dogs are a part of that.

Mads, too, appears to sometimes see unexplainable things. The most convincing of something perhaps paranormal happening was one evening about a month ago – it was late, and we were all in the sitting room. Mads suddenly began to stare at the wall above where Connor was sitting. He remained focused on the wall for ten minutes. At one point, I thought he might have been having a petit mal – style seizure, but we were able to distract him from whatever was happening several times; each time he was aware of us and immediately looked straight back to the place he was previously focused on. It was a little perturbing, but it hasn't happened since to that degree. Perhaps it was a shadow, or even a cobweb, who knows?

The three dogs have come so far in each of their journeys, and I feel so proud of them for how they have each conquered the challenges they've faced along their sometimes-dark roads. Out there can be a beautiful, loving world for animals, but likewise it can be the scariest place, among people who don't care.

I try to be optimistic and believe that things are getting better for animals; emotionally, it's been a long road for me, too. You can't work with animals and not be affected by the stories you become involved in, the tales of people's lives and the animals they love. You end up sharing in their joy and pain, on occasions becoming embroiled in the horror and sadness of situations when things don't work out. One thing I have learned, however, is that, for the most part, people are good, but when it does go wrong there can be the most terrible suffering of people and animals alike.

You don't take on a rescue dog without having this awareness in the back of your mind. There is always a possibility that the dog you adopt has experienced hurt, sadness, or tragedy. I think that with both Ralph and Mads a combination of these may have been the case.

Nell is messed up in other ways – I think through having experienced other dogs who have been aggressive towards her, she takes longer to accept strange dogs being around. The injuries she sustained before we got her didn't help either – not the injuries themselves, per se, but the time she spent away from other greyhounds and the people who were caring for her. Six weeks is a long time for a person to be in a hospital – both Alun and my brother were hospitalized for six weeks (Alun after a motorbike accident and Mark when a new kidney transplant failed). They both struggled emotionally and physically, and that was with having the ability to communicate with those around them. Dogs don't have that and must wait for their carers to notice their needs and, of course, they can't properly tell anyone how they feel. They also have no idea why they're there.

Who knows for sure what goes through the minds of the dogs we bring into our lives? I suppose the best we can do is to watch their body language and listen to the vocalizations our canine friends have evolved to use especially for their human companions. In doing so, we can try to interpret what they need from us. We have to discover what will make them happy and contented... and drive away the ghouls and monsters of their sleep. The nightmares don't matter anymore.

I used to say that in life there is one dog who gets inside your heart and soul and who you love so much more than the others who come along, and as I mentioned before, for me that dog was my old Jack. But each dog brings with them their courage, their joy, their needs, and their own self – and that is what gets inside you! And Ralph, well, Ralph fills my heart with the utmost love and happiness. I think Jack would be glad that a dog like Ralph picked up that baton.

I hope we have made Ralph feel happy and safe for all these years. He is a dog with the sweetest of hearts and he complements Nell and Mads so well. He is the rock on which both their foundations are built – he has shown them in his own Ralphie-way how to be around this strange species to which their people belong. In turn, we have finally found the true, and yet sometimes complex, Nell and Mads.

I love it when they are all around me, playing together, or relaxing. And I think of their stories and how they came to be here, and it gives me such joy that we could help them. I don't know why or how it was that these three dogs in particular happened to be here with us, as it could just as likely have been any other three rescue dogs, but something happened in the trajectories of our lives which resulted in our meeting them.

This road has not been smooth, and I'm sure there will be rumbles ahead, but they seem to be happy and content with how things ended up for them. And we are so glad they arrived here, all travelling along the same life path as we three humans.

And we love them.

Other books by Clare Cogbill

A Dog Like Ralph

… A Book for Anyone Who has Ever Loved a Rescue Dog

The true story of Ralph—a rescue dog with a difficult past—who loves other dogs, is frightened of people and cars, and mesmerized by cats, rabbits and 'Santa Please Stop Here' signs. Clare, his new human, tells with equal amounts of humour and sadness about the joys and challenges of having him as a companion.

His story is partly told through his eyes and describes how what he may have experienced before has affected how he interacts with those in his new 'forever' home. When Ralph's compatriots, Peggy, and Luella (Lucy to her friends), enter his life, it becomes clear that they have their own 'version of events' to add to the story!

Clare also writes about the pitfalls of a society that has resulted in Ralph being the way he is, and of how small changes could transform the plight of abandoned dogs.

This book is a tribute to the rescue dog.

A Dog Like Ralph gives some of the back story to The Diary of a Human and a Dog, A Dog Like Peggy, and Finding Nell and Mads, however it's not necessary to read it first.

The Diary of a Human and a Dog (or Three)

The story of a human and a dog sharing their unanticipated grief

When a dog loses their human companion, it results in the upheaval of everything they've ever loved. When a human loses their parent, it is the most heart-rending thing to have to deal with.

Lucy had been rescued just three years earlier and thought she had found her forever home. She was living as the sole dog in charge of an old woman. When the old woman passed away, Lucy found herself thrust into a life in which she would have to share her new humans with two other dogs. She had encountered Ralph and Peggy before and, quite frankly and in her stroppy terrier way, was not that keen on them.

This is the diary of Clare and Lucy. It is a story of how dogs can help humans heal, and how humans can help dogs to overcome their own very special sort of grief.

This book is Clare's most personal book as it focuses not only on the ways in which grief can affect us, but also on how dogs and people can help one another along the road to recovery. She wrote it in the time following her mother's unexpected death.

It could be read as Book 2 of the A Dog Like Ralph series, but essentially, they could be read in any order.

A Dog Like Peggy:
The Life and Times of a Rescued Greyhound

The book is narrated by Peggy the rescued greyhound, as she tells of her life on the tracks, and of the horrors she's witnessed. She also tells of the canine and human attachments she has made along the way.

She gives her (very frank) greyhound opinion of what she thinks about racing, the lot of a racing greyhound. Eventually, she shares her thoughts about the dogs she finally meets in her home that's forever – with Ralph and Lucy.

It is a heart-warming story because, after all, Peggy has been one of the luckier of these noble, gentle dogs.

Clare wrote this book (with Peggy, of course), in honour of all the racing greyhounds who are born into this cruel sport. She has a love for all dogs, and the plight of greyhounds touches her heart.

It could be read as Book 3 of the A Dog Like Ralph series, but essentially, they could be read in any order.

Fiction Books

This is the only fiction book so far, however there shall be more to follow.

Picture Me Now

An awkward, socially clumsy artist stumbles upon a possible connection between a stranger and a painting. Both become an obsession, threatening the life he has with his wife and daughter.

Does he have a connection with the woman? Will regression by a hypnotherapist provide the answers for which he is searching? And will that stop the dreams which are haunting his sleep?

Set against an environmental theme, this novel examines the concept of life after death, and whether connections could be re-established across lifetimes.

Perhaps there are times when we catch a glimpse of someone, and we know for sure deep in our heart that our worlds have been connected before. This book is for people who believe this to be possible.

It is also for those who question such things...

If you have enjoyed any of my books, a review on Goodreads and/or Amazon would be greatly appreciated.

If you'd like to get in touch, please find me on Facebook, Instagram, or my web page:

clarecogbill.com

*

I'd love to hear from you.

ABOUT THE AUTHOR

Clare Cogbill is the pen name of Julie McMorran. Julie is now a full-time writer, having spent her career working with animals and then teaching animal care and veterinary nursing.

She is a qualified RVN – Registered Veterinary Nurse, and in her early career worked for eleven years in veterinary surgeries – both rescue and general practice. She has an MSc. in Animal Welfare Science, Ethics and Law. In 2020, she retired from teaching after almost thirty years.

She loves all animals, and including this book, has written four dog books in all. After A Dog Like Ralph, she published The Diary of a Human and a Dog, a true story which explores grief and the human-animal bond. The other book is A Dog Like Peggy: The Life and Times of a Rescued Greyhound, in which her old dog Peggy narrated her own story about life on the tracks and finding her forever home.

Printed in Great Britain
by Amazon